LIVING
LIFE
TO THE
FULL

LIVING LIFE TO THE FULL

ANDRE BUTLER

CREATION
HOUSE
A STRANG COMPANY

LIVING LIFE TO THE FULL by Andre Butler
Published by Creation House
A Strang Company
600 Rinehart Road
Lake Mary, Florida 32746
www.creationhouse.com

Unless otherwise noted, all Scripture quotations are from the King James Version of the Bible.

Scripture quotations marked AMP are from the Amplified Bible. Old Testament copyright © 1965, 1987 by the Zondervan Corporation. The Amplified New Testament copyright © 1954, 1958, 1987 by the Lockman Foundation. Used by permission.

Scripture quotations marked NLT are from the Holy Bible, New Living Translation, copyright © 1996. Used by permission of Tyndale House Publishers, Inc., Wheaton, IL 60189. All rights reserved.

Word definitions from *Noah Webster's 1828 American Dictionary of the English Language*, Foundation for American Christians, reprint 1967. Also *Vine's Expository Dictionary of Old and New Testament Words*, Nashville, TN: Nelson, 1997.

Cover design by Terry Clifton

Library of Congress Control Number: 2007924900
International Standard Book Number: 978-1-59979-194-4

First Edition

07 08 09 10 11 — 987654321
Printed in the United States of America

CONTENTS

Chapter 1

LIFE TO THE FULL

The thief cometh not, but for to steal, and to kill,
and to destroy: I am come that they might have life,
and that they might have it more abundantly.
— John 10:10

LIFE IS INFINITELY valuable. The word itself comes from the Greek word *zoe* and means life in the absolute sense, life as God has it, eternal life, the God kind of life. This is the kind of life—we can call it *life to the full*—that Jesus came to give us. The Father sent Him on a mission to give us this life, and He left his heavenly estate to fulfill the Father's plan. After living thirty-three years here on earth, He was beaten and crucified. He gave His life to pay the price so we can have life.

When Jesus came to earth, He found a world of people who were suffering the awful effects of Satan's work to steal, kill, and destroy. Satan, the thief of John 10:10, tries to accomplish three things. First, he wants to steal from us the health, prosperity, and peace of mind that belong to us. Second, he wants to kill us. The Greek word translated "kill" in the New Testament means to rush or to breathe hard. It also means to sacrifice. If Satan cannot steal from us, he wants to huff and puff so that we will give up what belongs to us. He wants to intimidate us and scare us into letting it go. And third, he wants to destroy, and that word means to destroy fully.

Satan is all about causing God's people—and all people—harm. He wants to destroy every area of our lives. However, Jesus came that we might have life that produces blessings, which is the opposite of stealing, killing and destroying. Satan wants to steal from us, but Jesus restores. Satan wants to kill us, but Christ gives divine protection. Although Satan tries to intimidate us, God is by our side and says, "I've got your back." And even though Satan wants to destroy our lives, God prospers us and builds us up. As Psalm 115:14 says, "The Lord shall increase you more and more, you and your children."

Jesus came that you have life and that you might have it more abundantly. Did you notice the word *and*? After what we have just said about life, it would seem that having life is the be-all, the totality of all Jesus has to give. However, He added the promise of life "more abundantly." The Greek word translated "abundantly" means superabundant in quality, excessive, exceeding abundantly above. Jesus was saying that He came that you might have life, but I not just to have life. He wants you to have it in excess, beyond measure.

The English language is not as descriptive as the Greek language, and sometimes the Amplified Bible helps us understand what the original text was saying. For example, the

Amplified Bible states John 10:10 this way: "The thief comes only in order to steal and kill and destroy. I came that they may have and enjoy life, and have it in abundance (to the full, till it overflows)" (AMP). Jesus came for two reasons—that we might have life and that we might have life to the full. We as believers may have life, but not to the full. We may be saved, but our lives may not have any of the benefits of being saved. We may not be enjoying the overflow God wants us to enjoy.

If Jesus gave His life so we could have life to the full, we as believers must learn to live it that way. Suppose that someone gave us $10,000 to buy whatever we wanted. That would be wonderful unless we came back with only $3,000 worth of purchases and said, "Oh, that is all I really want. I am not really worthy to have the rest, and I'm tired." If we did this, we would have done our benefactor an injustice. They wanted to bless us with $10,000, but we turned away a large portion of what they gave us.

Let's think about what Jesus did for us. He made every good thing God has available to us. However, we as believers just take a little piece here, a little piece there. We may think we are not worthy to walk in the fullness of God's life or we may decide that we do not have the time to enter into it. This does God an injustice. He sent his Son so we could have life while we live here on this planet. He wanted us to have life—not to the quarter full, the half full, or the three-quarters full—but to the full.

I like the idea of living life to the full. I want to look at my life and see nothing broken and nothing missing. It is my desire to have a wonderful marriage and children who are blessed. What a joy it is to have a healthy body and healthy finances, to be out of debt and have my needs met. This kind of life gives me a full store to spread the Word more. Every time Satan comes against me, I can knock him out with the power of God. I like walking in divine protection and the wisdom of God. Yes, I desire to live life to the full.

God loves us, and He is faithful. If we will cooperate with Him, he will give us what we need and more. He is not El Cheapo. He is Jehovah Too Much. He is not a God who just gives you what you need. He is a God who will give us so much that we do not have enough room to receive it. We need to get this rooted in our heart because Satan wants to rob us of God's blessings. He will send thoughts, people, and circumstances our way to hinder us from receiving what God wants for us. However, when we hook our faith to God's promise of life to the full, He will bring it to pass.

Job 36:11, one of my favorite scriptures, says, "If they obey and serve him, they shall spend their days in prosperity, and their years in pleasures." If that offer is on the table, I want it. Too often we as Christians are dragging around one foot, barely making it through the day. Instead of this, we must learn how to walk; we must stop settling for less and be able to say, "I have nothing missing, nothing broken in my life. I am living life to the full."

The Source of Life

First John 5:11 says, "And this is the record, that God hath given to us eternal life, and this life is in his Son." Jesus came so we could have eternal life, and now that we have received Him as Lord of our lives, we have received it. Some people think they will receive eternal life when they get to heaven. However, when we receive Jesus, we are already living in our eternal life. God has already given it to us. We will never die spiritually.

When we look at the word "life," we think of a state of being. However, the Bible talks about it as more than that, as a spiritual substance or a spiritual force. Cartoons communicate very effectively by turning little creatures or little inanimate objects into people. For example, my daughter watches *Veggie Tales*, in which a little tomato called Bob and a cucumber called Larry teach the Word to children. We can learn from this to look at life not just as something we have, but as a person, a substance that will do something for us. The life is in Jesus Christ, God's Son.

John 1:4 speaks about this when it says of Jesus, "In him was life." It is not just that he had life, it was in him, in His spirit. John 5:26 also testifies that "the Father hath life in himself." His very nature is life. He has life in Him. What would God's life look like if He came to earth? To answer that question we only have to look at Jesus' life. God did come to the earth. As we look at the life of Jesus, we see that He lived life to the full. He walked in protection, in wealth, in health, in victory. Satan never got a hand up on Jesus until He surrendered himself according to the Father's will.

Jesus became poor at the same time He became sin, sick, and ultimately a curse (Gal. 3:13). Then He went to the cross. He lived His life on the Earth as a man in covenant with God who enjoyed the full benefits of obeying that covenant, which includes being "plenteous in goods" and the lender versus the borrower (Deut. 1–2; 11–12). An in-depth look at Jesus' life finds Him not homeless (John 1:38–39) and lacking, but prospering.

(See Matthew 2:11; not just three men and inexpensive gifts; Luke 8:1–3; Matthew 17:27.)

First John 5:12 promises, "He that hath the Son hath life." If we have the Son, we have the life of God within us. We already have everything that is available—all the equipment, all the resources, everything we need to succeed in every area of life. This means that we have life right now. We have the life of God—the nature of God—inside us right now, and it is there to produce something. When we received Jesus, the life of God came into us and made us new creatures. Since then, it has been producing life more abundantly.

God does not want us to have the mentality that we get saved and then hang on while we fight the devil and suffer here on earth. The belief that we will only get what God has for us when we get to heaven is unscriptural. We have the life of God within us now, and it is there to produce all that He has for us here before we go to heaven. God wants us to enjoy this life and prosper right now.

We are residents of this world, a place with inclement weather and roads that are in disrepair. However, we are citizens of the kingdom of heaven. Our home, the heavenly city, is 144,000 miles high, wide, and long. Its foundations are made of precious stones, and every gate is made out of one pearl. It has streets of gold. A river flows out of the throne of God and runs through the city. This glorious place is where we are from. When we made Jesus Lord of our lives, God made us a new creation. We are citizens of heaven and have heaven's privileges available to us while we are here on earth. God wants us to enjoy them to the full.

In John 10:9, Jesus says, "I am the door: by me if any man

enter in, he shall be saved, and shall go in and out, and find pasture." Jesus is describing people as if they are sheep, and His words point us back to Psalm 23:

> The LORD is my shepherd; I shall not want [I will not lack]. He maketh me to lie down in green pastures: he leadeth me beside the still waters.... Yea, though I walk through the valley of the shadow of death, I will fear no evil: for thou art with me; thy rod and thy staff they comfort me. Thou preparest a table before me in the presence of mine enemies [I am more blessed than they are]: thou anointest my head with oil; my cup runneth over. Surely goodness and mercy shall follow me all the days of my life.

This is not a psalm about heaven. The shadow of death is not in heaven, and there are surely no enemies there. No, this psalm is talking about life on earth. It says that when we follow the shepherd, God will cause us to lay in green pastures, not brown pastures or food stamp pastures. He will lead us beside still waters, not hurricanes. He will protect us in the presence of our enemies. They will see us being blessed and they will be angry. However, they will know that God is real. And all the days of our lives, everywhere we go, we have twins—goodness and mercy—following us. This is what Christ means when he says we will find pasture. This is how he wants us to live.

The Provision of Spiritual Blessings

Grace be to you, and peace, from God our Father, and from the Lord Jesus Christ. Blessed be the God and Father of our Lord Jesus Christ, who hath blessed us with all spiritual blessings in heavenly places.

—Ephesians 1:2–3

Grace and peace are spiritual blessings that come from God. We do not automatically receive them because we live on this planet. However, when we receive Jesus, we receive life and all spiritual blessings. The word "spiritual" means non-carnal and refers to any blessings that come from God. We might call them divine blessings.

God has given us all divine blessings—health, protection, wisdom. If we are believing in God for a mate, we already have one. If something is good, it is from God, and we already own it. When we are born again, we are delivered from the power of darkness and are brought into the kingdom of light (Col. 1:13). We are adopted into the kingdom of God and receive everything He owns. He gives us everything that He is, everything that is good. It is already in our name. And why not? Romans 8:32 says, "He that spared not his own Son, but delivered him up for us all, how shall he not with him also freely give us all things?"

Galatians 3:13 says that Christ has redeemed us from the curse of law. He has set us free from poverty, sickness, and spiritual death. How did he do it? He was made a curse for us when He hung on the cross. Second Corinthians 5:21 explains, "For he hath made him to be sin for us, who knew no sin; that we might be made the righteousness of God in him." Second Corinthians 8:9 adds that He was made poor so we might be rich. And Isaiah 53 teaches us that He was made sick so we might be healed. (See Isaiah 53:4–5, 10; the word *griefs* refers to sickness, and *sorrows* refers to pains in the original Hebrew.) And all this happened two thousand years ago.

First Peter 2:24 says, "By whose [Christ's] stripes ye were healed." When Jesus suffered His stripes, we received our healing. We were not even here yet, but God knew we would be. When Jesus died on the cross, He paid the price for us to have all spiritual blessings. He laid up healing, riches, righteousness, victory, protection, wisdom, a prosperous marriage, and mighty children in our own safe deposit box. We can come and possess these blessings whenever we want. We can enjoy life to the full.

God knew we would receive Him, and He prepared all spiritual blessings for us before we were born. First Corinthians 2:9 says, "Eye hath not seen, nor ear heard...the things which God hath prepared for them that love him." Whatever we need, we already have. It is already ours. It is already in our name. We are already more than a conqueror. However, we need to know where our blessings are and how to get them.

As Ephesians 1:3 says, God has "blessed us with all spiritual blessings in heavenly places." The word *heavenly* means spiritual; it is referring to the spirit realm. As Christians we have all spiritual blessings laid up for us in the spirit realm. However, many of us do not know it. For example, the body of Christ has been fighting for years over whether God wants us to be healed. When we understand that we must listen to what the Bible says, we realize that we do have all that God has prepared for us. Then we have to learn how to withdraw His blessings to be able to live life to the full.

How to Withdraw Our Blessings

God is the ultimate planner. He sees the end from the beginning and knows what we are going to need ten thousand years before we need it. And he has already provided for it. As Bishop Keith Butler once said, "God has pre-vision. So he gives you provision." God has laid up all spiritual blessings for us in our own account. Whatever we need has already been paid for, and it is available. We can understand this when we see parents save money for their children's college education. Even though their children are very young and have no interest in college, these parents know that their children will go to college one day. They look ahead and make provisions for them.

God has already provided everything we need to live life to the full, but we have to learn how to withdraw it. God gives us instruction for this in 2 Peter 1:2–4:

> Grace and peace be multiplied unto you through the knowledge of God, and of Jesus our Lord, According as his divine power hath given unto us all things that pertain unto life and godliness...Whereby are given unto us exceeding great and precious promises: that by these ye might be partakers of the divine nature.

This verse, like Ephesians 1:2, extends the blessings of grace and peace. God must want us to have grace and peace. The Greek word for *grace* means graciousness and is translated "benefit." Many times this word is used in Scripture to refer to the anointing. The word *peace* means prosperity, and it is translated as "rest" and to "set at one again." It means to be in a position where we have nothing missing and nothing broken. God wants that for us. That is living life to the full.

Peter says that grace and peace are multiplied to us. We know that they already belong to us, but now we learn how to withdraw them—"through the knowledge of God, and of Jesus our Lord." The word "knowledge," which comes from the Greek word *epignosis*, does not mean natural knowledge. It refers to revelation knowledge, full knowledge or full discernment. This is the kind of knowledge Peter received when he confessed that Jesus was the Christ, the Son of the living God, in Matthew 16:15–17. We need this revelation knowledge.

As Peter continues, He gives us the withdrawal form to receive grace and peace. He explains that God has given us great promises to use to "be partakers of the divine nature." The word *nature* has a number of meanings—growth, natural production, native disposition, state of being. We can have a divine state of being, life as God has it. We can have life to the full.

We need to know what God has promised us. In John 15:7 Jesus said, "If ye abide in me, and my words abide in you, ye shall ask what ye will, and it shall be done unto you." Ephesians 6:2-3 teaches, "Honour thy father and mother; which is the first commandment with promise; That it may be well with thee, and thou mayest live long on the earth." Psalm 103:3-5 identifies some of God's benefits: He forgives all our iniquities; He heals all our diseases; He redeems our life from destruction; and He satisfies our mouth with good things.

God has a promise for everything in life. He has given us all things, but we have to use His promises to gain access to them. When we look at our lives and see lack in an area, we need to come to the Bible and find where God has promised provision for that. It is not good enough to just quote Scripture. We need to open the Bible, read the Scriptures, and create a list of scriptures. And we need revelation knowledge of God's promises. They have to be real to us on the inside.

As I sat in a barber shop one day, I was thinking about my response to some physical problems, an area where Satan has tried to attack me. The Lord spoke to me, "The only reason you are sick is because you will not do what it takes to get you healed. It makes no sense for you to continue to be sick. Why don't you just do what it takes to get your healing?" I had heard that before, but at that moment it was revelation.

Many times we do not receive from God because we do not want to study His promises in our area of need. That is how it was with me. I could study prosperity and victory and protection all day long. However, I needed healing more than anything, and my failure to study it was keeping me from living life to the full. The Lord told me, "That is what you need, so just get in it."

So I began studying God's promises to heal. I have healing tapes and healing CD's in my car, and I have a long list of healing scriptures and a healing devotional. I am reading a healing book all the time. When I began to expose myself to these things, I had some faith in God's promises. Now, however, I am like a rock in it. I know that healing belongs to me. And I know I am healed.

Revelation comes like the lights come on. We see something in Scripture and say, "Oh." It should happen every time we come to church. Through revelation, we have faith like a rock, and our heart is fixed. We have peace that passes understanding when we face desperate situations. It is does not matter what is happening. We know we have what God has promised. Philippians 4:19 promises, "My God shall supply all [my] need[s]." And Isaiah 54:17 declares, "No weapon that is formed against [me] shall prosper."

We have to force ourselves to study what the word of God says about our needs. We must press in and take hold of what God has for us. That is how we will be able to live life to the full. Teaching on God's promises is available at many churches and bookstores. If we are lacking, it is because we have not been diligent to act on the opportunities to receive revelation and withdraw our blessings.

If we live life to the full, it will impact not only us but also the world around us for Jesus. Our witness is damaged when we try to witness to people and they see that we are sick or poor. Our witness is less effective if people see that our marriages or our families are not healthy. We may talk about receiving Jesus, but all they hear is the message to be like us. It means nothing to them if they are doing just as well as us and having fun doing it.

We need to live life to the full. God's will for us, the church, is that we be blessed above the people of this world. The only way that will happen is for us to receive revelation of the promises God gave us and then act on it.

Activating God's Promises

Jesus made provision for all of us to be whole, and it really should not take us long to arrive at wholeness in our salvation. This is what the early Christians experienced. Their lives were all about Jesus. The Bible says that they had no lack (Acts 4:34), and people either walked in health or received their healing (John 5:14–15). Their biggest problem was persecution.

Because we do not live the lifestyle of the early Christians, we do not get the results they experienced. The Bible tells us to meditate on the word of God day and night, but most Christians do not do this. Every time we skip the Word, we miss out on revelation and wisdom. Every time we skip prayer, we forfeit anointing. We need to recognize this and seek God in His Word and in prayer.

When we do this, Satan will attack us and try to deceive us into thinking, "It gets worse every time I touch the Bible, so I am just going to leave it alone. Bad things happen every time I come to church so I am just not coming." We have to fight against these thoughts and learn how to rebuke the enemy. We must choose to only think and speak what the Word says. One way we can do this is through praise. As we praise God for what he has already done for us and believe he is going to change our situations, we will see God move. Because of our faith expressed through praise, God is able to come into our lives and fulfill His promises.

In times of spiritual battle, we may find that Satan has a stronghold in our lives. He is an outlaw, and he may take up residence in our body, our finances, or our marriage. Strongholds may have developed when we were sinners or because of bad habits. They have been in our families for generations. However, God desires to speak to us through His Word and reprogram and change these areas of our lives.

In Mark 11:24, Jesus says, "Therefore I say unto you, What things soever ye desire, when ye pray, believe that ye receive them, and ye shall have them." He invites us to pray for whatever we desire—healing, wealth, victory. And then He says that we are to believe that we took possession of them at that moment. To believe is to be firmly persuaded, totally confident even though we do not see the desired result. We are to believe that what we need is already in our lives. Even though we do not see it or feel it, God says to believe it.

It may seem that nothing has changed, but we walk, as 2 Corinthians 5:7 says, "by faith, not by sight." We have to learn to shut our eyes to the circumstances, and open our eyes to what God said. We have to make a decision to believe that we have that promise, that grace, that peace, that wisdom in our lives right now. And then we have to keep believing it until it shows up. This is the faith of God, by which we speak to our mountains. In Mark 11:23 Jesus promises that when we speak to our mountains to be removed, they will be cast into the sea. It will be as if they never existed. This is one of God's exceedingly great promises.

This is life as God has it. God told some ravens that there was a prophet of God living by the brook Cherith that they needed to bring bread and meat twice a day (1 Kings 17). And they did it. God spoke to the sun to explain that His people were fighting a battle down there, and Joshua needed help. He commanded the sun to stop for a moment. And the sun did it (Josh. 10). How many times did God say something and it was so? God says we can live life like He lives life. Whatever you bind on earth will be bound in heaven. Whatever you loose on earth will be loosed in heaven. And, yes, whatever mountain you speak to will be removed. This is the promise of God.

But how do we activate God's promises? It does not matter

how we feel or how things look. God is a rewarder of those who come to Him in prayer. He does not hold anything back. In Genesis 17:4, when Abraham was ninety-nine years old, God told him, I am going to make you a father of many nations. His wife, Sarah, who could not have a child, was ninety. Abraham, the Bible said, reached a place where he kept looking at what God said. He was strong in faith and gave God glory (Rom. 4:20). Abraham did not have an instant manifestation, and many times we do not. But once we have the revelation of God's promises, His Word in us, we come to God in prayer and trust that we already have His blessing and provision. This is how we receive what God has promised and live life to the full.

We must pray, "Father, I asked for this. I thank you. I have it right now." It may seem that all we are doing is going to bed, getting up, and praising God. Yet all this time God is bringing it to pass. It may be first the blade, then the ear, then the full corn in the ear (Mark 4:28), but it is coming. As long as we keep our faith, as long as we keep praising God and believing that we already have it, it is coming. Our thoughts, words and actions have to say, "I already have it." Satan will send thoughts that we cannot meditate on God's promise. However, we have to audibly say, "I rebuke that, Satan. You are misinformed. I already have it."

When we take these actions, we receive God's blessings. His will is that we allow Him to keep every single promise He has given us. We can live life to the full.

Chapter 2

CHOOSING THE PLACE OF REST

These things have I spoken unto you, being yet present with you. But the Comforter, which is the Holy Ghost, whom the Father will send in my name, he shall teach you all things, and bring all things to your remembrance, whatsoever I have said unto you.
—John 14:25–26

THE NIGHT BEFORE His death, Jesus sat down with his disciples at what is called the Last Supper. After Judas Iscariot left the table to act on his plan to betray Him, Jesus told the remaining eleven that He would not be with them much longer. He began to give them instructions for how they should live after He left and promised that the Holy Spirit would come and teach them all things.

John 16:22 says that the disciples were sorrowful.

They had become accustomed to walking with the Savior, the Messiah, the Christ for three and a half years, and their every need had been met. They had seen Him do supernatural things they probably never expected to see. In addition, Jesus had put His anointing on them, and they went out and did the same works He did. Luke 9:1–2 and 10:1–20 tell how He gave them authority and power to heal the sick and cast out devils. The disciples had received the benefits of Jesus' earthly ministry, and the truths He taught them had changed their lives. But now he said he was leaving.

Jesus knew that God had a great mission for His disciples to accomplish to make disciples of all nations (Matt. 28:19, AMP). However, how could they do this if Jesus was not going to be with them? Jesus began His answer to this question by saying, "But the Comforter, which is the Holy Ghost…" (John 14:26). We may face trouble, "but God." He is bigger than our problems, our circumstances, our difficulties. He is more than able to bring us through to surpassing victory. We are not just conquerors, but "more than conquerors" (Rom. 8:37). We do not just barely squeak by; we blow the enemy out because of God!

The Holy Ghost or the Holy Spirit as we know Him is the third person of the Godhead. We know that God is one, and yet He is three different persons. Sometimes people have a problem trying to understand this, but we can compare it to a basketball team with twelve players. The team is one, but it is twelve different persons. They all wear the same name on their jersey, but they all have different roles to play. Using this comparison, we recognize that God the Father has a role. God the Son has His role, and at the time of the Last Supper, He was about to complete His assignment. It was time for God the Holy Spirit to step in.

It is important to notice that the Godhead is holy. The Father says, "Be ye holy; for I am holy" (1 Pet. 1:16). The Bible says that Jesus was without sin (Heb. 4:15); He was holy. And the Word of God calls the Holy Spirit "holy." We have to remember that He lives inside us and we have to learn how to treat Him as He is, a holy guest. When a pastor visits people in their homes, they sometimes act differently than usual because they consider him a reverend, a holy guest. They want to do what they think is right in his eyes. The Holy Spirit always lives in us, and we need to treat Him like a holy guest. If we would not do something in front of a pastor, we should not do it in front of the Holy Spirit.

Jesus said the Father would send the Holy Spirit. As this implies, the Holy Spirit had an assignment, a mission. He came from heaven with a mission, and part of it was to "teach [us] all things." The Holy Spirit has come to teach us, and He is teaching all the time in many ways. We have our own personal tutor. Because this is true, we must ask ourselves if we have been receiving His lessons.

In John 16:12–13 Jesus told His disciples:

> I have yet many things to say unto you, but ye cannot bear them now. Howbeit when he, the Spirit of truth, is come, he will guide you into all truth: for he shall not speak of himself; but whatsoever he shall hear, that shall he speak: and he will shew you things to come.

Even though He had been teaching His disciples for three and a half years, Jesus had more to tell them. However, because they were not ready, He promised to send the Holy Spirit so He could continue to teach them. He said, "I am going to speak through Him and tell you what I have to say" (author's paraphrase). In other words, He explained that the Holy Spirit will, in a sense, be a mediator who brings us to a place of *all* truth.

First Timothy 2:4 says it is the will of God that all men be saved and come unto the knowledge of the truth. The Amplified Bible talks about progressively coming up to truth, like climbing a stairway. We start off with the truth about Jesus as Lord and Savior, but under the teaching of the Holy Spirit and by the will of God we continue to walk with Jesus and increase in knowledge. As the Holy Spirit brings us up the stairway, we learn more and more about the kingdom of God.

We as believers are in the school of the Holy Spirit. When we meet as a church, the Holy Spirit uses some of us to teach the Word of God so we can come unto the knowledge of the truth. The more we know, the more God can do for us and through us. God wants us to know all things, all spiritual truths. For this reason, we must not limit our study of the God's Word. Sometimes we have no problem studying faith and prosperity and healing, but do not want anything to do with Bible prophecy. However, at least one third of the Bible is prophecy and it is the will of God that we have a full understanding of it.

God wants us to know *all* things. He wants us to know the length, the depth, the breadth and the height of His love (Eph. 3:18–19). He wants us to know all there is of Him. This will happen as we consistently spend time in His Word at home and at church. God wants us to have a full understanding of the kingdom of God because it will serve us well in this life and also in the life to come. The more we learn and grow, the more we will prosper and the more we will produce.

In John 14:26 Jesus promises His disciples that the Holy Spirit will remind them of what He had said. That is how we got the gospels. How could the writers of the Gospels be so detailed? The Holy Spirit brought Jesus' words to their remembrance. And how could Paul's writings be right in line with what Jesus said? The Holy Spirit taught Paul what Jesus had wanted to say. The Holy Spirit is like a thread that runs through all of Scripture.

The Holy Spirit is our teacher. This means that we cannot come to church with the mentality that we know it all already. We need to listen to the ministry of the Word no matter who is teaching. Even if we have been saved for fifty years, God still has revelation for us to receive. When we reach a certain stage of spiritual maturity and hear the title of a message, we are tempted to say, "Ah, I already know about this." Yes, the speaker may say exactly what you expect, but the Spirit of God will include a nugget that will bless you and bring to another level.

God uses people to teach other people, and we need to approach the Word correctly, no matter who is teaching. For example, God can give us revelation when we read Bible stories to a three-year-old child. The Holy Spirit will teach us all the time because He lives in us for that purpose. Although we may want to pick what lessons He teaches, we need to allow Him to teach us whatever He wants. Our place is to be willing students who say, "Teach me, Holy Spirit." David said, "The law of thy mouth is better than thousands of gold and silver" (Ps. 119:72). We need to approach God's Word like a buried treasure. If we give proper attention to it, God will reveal it to us by the Holy Spirit.

The Invitation to Come and Rest

Ho, every one that thirsteth, come ye to the waters, and he that hath no money; come ye, buy, and eat; yea, come, buy wine and milk without money and without price. Wherefore do ye spend money for that which is not bread? and your labour for that which satisfieth not? hearken diligently unto me and eat ye that which is good, and let your soul delight itself in fatness. Incline your ear, and come unto me: hear, and your soul shall live."

—Isaiah 55:1–3

God knows all things. He knows everything we need to be all that He wants us to be and all that we want to be. He sent the Holy Spirit to teach us and has invited us to come and listen to His instruction. We have the assurance that when we seek God for direction, He will not withhold it from us. He gives to all men freely and tells us that the only thing you need to do is ask in faith. When you seek Him, you will find Him."

For my thoughts are not your thoughts, neither are your ways my ways, saith the LORD. For as the heavens are higher than the earth, so are my ways higher than your ways, and my thoughts than your thoughts. For as the rain cometh down, and the snow from heaven, and returneth not thither, but watereth the earth, and maketh it bring forth and bud, that it may give seed to the sower, and bread to the eater: So shall my word be that goeth forth out of my mouth: it shall not return unto me void, but it shall accomplish that which I please, and it shall prosper in the thing whereto I sent it. For ye shall go out with joy, and be led forth with peace: the mountains and the hills shall break forth before you into singing, and all the trees of the field shall clap their hands."

—Isaiah 55:8–12

As the prophet Isaiah said, "God's thoughts are not our thoughts, and His ways are not our ways." This, however, does not mean that we will never know what God wants us to know and do. Rather, God has instructed us to forget our way and forget our thoughts. His are much better and much higher than ours, He gave you His Word so we can know His thoughts and His ways. Come and enjoy peace and walk in the life He wants us to live.

All things are delivered unto me of my Father: and no man knoweth the Son, but the Father; neither knoweth any man the Father, save the Son, and he to whomsoever the Son will reveal him. Come unto me, all ye that labour and are heavy laden, and I will give you rest. Take my yoke upon you, and learn of me; for I am meek and lowly in heart: and ye shall find rest unto your souls. For my yoke is easy and my burden is light."

—Matthew 11:27–30

The Son reveals the Father to people, and as we have seen, He does this through the Holy Spirit. As He described His relationship to the Father, Jesus invited us to come and receive rest and refreshing. He promised that we would receive rest by taking His yoke, which is easy, upon us. And what is His yoke? It's His teaching.

The Spirit of God speaks to us today and asks us to allow ourselves to be taught through His Word and His leading and guiding. He will teach you through men and women of God if you incline your ear and receive what He has to say. We must come not only to church, but to the Book. When you come in prayer and let Him minister to you, you will find that you will have refreshing. You will have rest unto your souls; that heavy burden will be lifted off you. All your struggling will not be there any more and you will find that your life is what it should be.

We will not find rest for our souls until we make God's Word part of our daily lives. Just as we practice daily habits of good hygiene to be successful in life, we also need to come daily to the Word of God and to allow Him to teach us. In addition, it is important that we receive the ministry of His Word from others. I partner with a ministry that God uses to reveal truth I need to hear. And God has called us to come and receive from His Word at church. If we allow the Holy Spirit to be our teacher, He will give us what we need. We will find that His yoke is easy, His burden is light and there is rest for our souls.

In Jesus' ministry, the multitudes came to hear and be healed. And today, the hearing of the Word comes before the manifestation of His glory the vast majority of the time. The Holy Spirit has already prepared the food of His Word and set it on the table. He has provided truth for every situation we face. He offers to teach you about your business, your industry, how to be a good husband and wife, and how to raise your kids. If we come and receive His ministry we will not miss out on the rest (Heb. 4:1–13) and refreshing (Acts 3:19) He has for us.

The Place of Rest

Now it came to pass, as they went, that he entered into a certain village: and a certain woman named Martha received him into her house. And she had a sister called Mary, which also sat at Jesus' feet, and heard his word. But Martha was cumbered about much serving, and came to him, and said, "Lord, dost thou not care that my sister hath left me to serve alone? bid her therefore that she help me." And Jesus answered and said unto her, Martha, Martha, thou art careful and troubled about many things. But one thing is needful: and Mary hath chosen that good part, which shall not be taken away from her.

—Luke 10:38–42

The story of Jesus' visit to the home of Martha and Mary in Luke 10 illustrates the important truth that nothing should cause us to be so busy that we do not seek God through the ministry of His Word. Mary was sitting at Jesus' feet and listening to His teaching. Martha, however, who was busy serving, became very bothered because Mary was not helping her and interrupted Jesus as He taught. "Don't you care that I am doing all this work, and she is not doing anything?" she asked.

Jesus replied by going deeper than the situation at hand and speaking into her whole life. He identified that there were a lot of things going wrong for her, and that what she needed was rest for her soul.

Mary had chosen the place of rest by coming and sitting under Jesus' teaching. This was the one thing Jesus identified as "needful" for Martha. Although it was a good thing for Martha to give herself to serving, Jesus' words to her show the importance of our priorities. Even when God has told us to do something for Him, He is not going to take us away from the table of his Word. That is our sustenance! However, we can become so busy serving in the church that we never sit down to hear the Word. When this happens, we forget why we are serving. Our attitudes turn negative, our relationships suffer, and we may fall into sin.

When we look at this story with natural thinking, it appears that Martha was right and Mary was being lazy. However, spiritual thinking is different, as Jesus showed by His response to Martha. He did not criticize Mary for sitting and listening to Him. Instead He said that she had chosen the good part, which would "not be taken away from her." She was allowing Jesus to teach her, and her life would be blessed.

We, like Mary, need to choose the place of rest and sit under the teaching of God's Word. We need to allow the Holy Spirit to be our teacher by showing up for class every day and studying what He wants to teach us. This is the pill God has provided for every illness. It does not matter if we have AIDS, cancer, a backache, or a headache. It does not matter if we struggle with depression or financial needs. When we receive the ministry of God's Word, it changes us. God builds up our faith so that it works in our areas of need. As we continue to seek Him and His Word, He keeps changing us and giving us more positive results.

The ministry of God's Word is not the kind of pill we take only one time. If we only come to church on Sunday every once in a while, we cannot expect things to change. We have to keep taking this pill for life. Jesus said we should live by the Word of God. When we miss it a few times, we are going to lack. If we miss it frequently, we are going to lack more. We have to keep receiving the Word every day. When we are really struggling in an area, we have to stay at it. God wants to take our weaknesses and make them our strengths.

We might say, "Ah, I am already in my Word." But are we "careful and troubled" about anything? We may be struggling with a difficult situation, a stronghold we have not been able to overcome, a need to walk in holiness. The answer is a steady diet of the Word of God for our area of need. Some people have a hard time believing this. They forget that the ministry of God's Word changes us. They forget that God reveals answers for our needs and sets us free from the things that trouble us. When we hear the teaching of the Word at church, we walk out with full hearts.

Sometimes we forget this if we have been Christians for a while. However, the Word of God is pregnant with revelation, and God wants us to constantly receive all that He has for us. He wants to help us live life to the full, and He may bring us to the Gospel of John, the Old Testament, the Book of Revelation, or the Epistles. The Scriptures are rich and full. I can read something I have already marked because it ministered to me before, and receive a new revelation that changes my life.

God the Holy Spirit does not just want to teach us. He also wants us to teach others. Because we have allowed Him to teach us, we have something that we can teach others when the Holy Spirit opens the door. In Mark 13:11, Jesus tells His disciples that the Holy Spirit would give them the words they should say when they needed them. As we listen to Him, the Holy Spirit will tell us when to witness and what to say. He will tell us what to say when we help others become established in the faith.

He will help us teach others—including our family members—so they can grow up spiritually. The teaching ministry of the Holy Spirit is awesome, and we can receive it and participate in it.

Chapter 3

DELIGHTFUL LIVING

*Trust in the LORD, and do good; so shalt thou
dwell in the land, and verily thou shalt be fed.
Delight thyself also in the LORD: and he shall give
thee the desires of thine heart.*
—Psalm 37:3–4

THE WILL OF God is that we receive the desires of our hearts. Psalm 37:3 teaches us to trust in the Lord and do good. We cannot walk in the fullness of what God wants us to have unless we have faith in God and do good works. As we practice these things, He will provide for us and bless us. And, as verse 4 reveals, He will give us the desires of our hearts as we delight ourselves in Him. He promises not just one desire, but the "desires" of our hearts.

The word *delight* includes the word *light*. When something good happens to someone, we may observe that his

29

face lights up as light seems to come from inside him. While God wants us to have continual joy that causes us to light up, He also tells us: "Delight yourself," turn your own light on. Do not wait for good news to cause you to rejoice. This is *your* responsibility. He expects you to cause yourself to delight. We can choose to delight in God and rejoice in Him at any time. Philippians 4:4 says, "Rejoice in the Lord always: and again I say, Rejoice."

First Samuel 30 tells how David and his men returned to their home in Ziklag and found that it had been raided by the Amalekites and burned. As if that wasn't bad enough, the enemy had also taken their families captive. David's men were so distressed that they were talking about stoning him. Of course, David had lost some of his family, as well. But the Bible teaches that David did not allow himself to have a "pity party," as we might call it. No, he encouraged himself in the Lord.

This story shows us that we have the ability to change our emotional state, no matter what is going on around us. We can decide that we are not going to be depressed, sad, or bad. We can choose not to give the devil pleasure, but to rejoice in the Lord always. We can encourage ourselves in the Lord and delight in Him. The Hebrew word translated "delight" means to be soft or pliable, luxurious. It is also translated to "sport self." I can identify with this because I enjoy and delight myself in watching the Detroit Lions play on television. It is what I have chosen to do.

We are like children who are standing outside a toy store and cannot get in because it is locked. We need a key so we can open the door and go in and play with whatever we desire. The psalmist says, "Delight thyself also in the Lord." He does not tell us to delight ourselves in things such as sports or shopping, although it is not wrong to enjoy them. But he says that the key to receiving all the desires of our hearts is that we delight ourselves in the Lord above all else. Only the Lord has the will, the way, and the anointing to give us all our desires.

God wants us to enjoy the desires of our hearts and to lack no good thing. This, of course, is based on the premise that we are not going to ask for anything outside His will, which is full of good things. God designed us and created us. He made each of us unique, one of a kind, and there is no one else like you or me. He placed our desires within us, and they go right along with His blueprint for us. Since this is true, God knows the desires of our hearts. Matthew 6:8 says that God knows what we need even before we ask Him. He knows your desires, and it is his will to give them to us. If that were not true, we would not have the master key of Psalm 37:4.

God's Idea of Delightful Living

If ye abide in me, and my words abide in you, ye shall ask what ye will, and it shall be done unto you.
—John 15:7

This is God's idea of what I like to call delightful living. He said that when we abide in Him and His Words abide in us, we can ask the Father what we will. God will hear what we ask and then He will say, "Done." Our desire will be met because His heart, His desire is to see us enjoy our desires.

Only God can give us the desires of our hearts. We may get a few things we desire from the world if we pay a price, but we will never receive all that we desire. For example, the world may give us money, but only God can give us wholeness. God has a long menu of things He desires to give us, and He says that He will give them to you if you will just delight in Him. He offers us wealth or health or prosperity in our relationships, a promotion on the job, victory over trouble, and divine protection.

As we delight in God, we can choose whatever we want from God's menu and He will meet our desires. First John 5:14-15 says, "This is the confidence that we have in him, that, if we ask any thing according to his will, he heareth us: And if we know that he hear us, whatsoever we ask, we know that we have the petitions that we desired of him." Second Peter 1:4 teaches that God has given us "exceeding great and precious promises" that we can partake of the divine nature. We can walk in the fullness of abundant life.

The Bible repeats the key for Godly success over and over. It may be presented in different ways such as delighting in God or living for Him. However, God just keeps saying it. As he summed it up in Psalm 37:4, if we just delight ourselves in the Lord, we can have all the desires of our hearts. This includes not only what we need but also whatever we desire—to be pain-free, to walk, to receive the mate God has for us if we are single. Whatever it is, we can have it!

God wants you to have what you will. He wants you to have the desires of your heart. First Timothy 6:17 teaches that God "giveth us richly all things to enjoy." Isaiah 1:19 promises that if we are willing and obedient we will "eat the good of the land." We are going to enjoy the good. And Ecclesiastes 5:18–20 also helps us see the heart of God:

Behold that which I have seen: it is good and comely [beautiful] for one to eat and to drink, and to enjoy the good of all his labour that he taketh under the sun all the days of his life, which God giveth him: for it is his portion. Every man also to whom God hath given riches and wealth, and hath given him power to eat thereof [enjoy the benefits of it] and to take his portion, and to rejoice in his labour; this is the gift of God. For he shall not much remember the days of his life; because God answereth him in the joy of his heart.

This scripture shows that God likes to watch us enjoy ourselves. As James 1:17 explains that every good thing, every perfect gift comes from Him. The statement "God answereth him in the joy of his heart" from the passage above refers to a request or petitions, the meaning for the word "desire" in Psalm 37:4. It reveals that this person was so blessed because God was answering him in the joy of his heart. God has given him the desires of his heart and his life is so blessed he hardly remembers his days. He has forgotten about the good thing that happened last week, because he is too busy enjoying the good thing that is happening now.

When God looks at people like this, he calls it good and beautiful. It is His gift to those who will serve Him. Psalm 35:27 says that God takes pleasure "in the prosperity of his servant." He enjoys it when we enjoy ourselves. He is a giver, and a liberal one at that. James 1:5 says, "If any of you lack wisdom [this applies to any area of lack], let him ask of God, that giveth to all men liberally, and upbraideth not; and it shall be given him." This is one revelation that we as believers need to receive. We tend to picture God as stingy. However, when we look at God's Word, we see that He gives freely and liberally.

God wants to give us His many blessings, but He is waiting for us to get in position to receive. Second Chronicles 16:9 says that "the eyes of the LORD run to and fro throughout the whole earth, to shew himself strong in the behalf of them whose heart is perfect toward him." In Malachi 3:10 God says that when we give Him the tithe and the offering, He "will...open you the windows of heaven." The Hebrew meaning for this promise is, "I will empty out" a blessing on you. Yes, God is giving. The question is, are we in position to receive? People who enjoy God's gifts have learned to receive from Him.

God Wants *Our* Joy to Be Full

And in that day ye shall ask me nothing. Verily, verily, I say unto you, Whatsoever ye shall ask the Father in my name, he will give it you. Hitherto have ye asked nothing in my name: ask, and ye shall receive, that your joy may be full.

—John 16:23–24

When Jesus said this to His disciples, He was nearing the end of His earthly ministry and quickly approaching His crucifixion the next day. As He was completing His last instructions to His disciples, He told them to ask God—something they hadn't done yet—in order to receive.

Why did Jesus say this? John 8:28 says that Jesus spoke what the Father taught Him. And Hebrews 1:3 teaches that Jesus was "the express image" of God on earth. If Jesus did something, it was the Father who did it. If Jesus said something, it was the Father who said it. Because this is true, we know that on this night before Jesus' death, God the Father was looking at the disciples who had been following Jesus for three and a half years. Speaking through the words of Jesus, He told them that they had been delighting in Him, but had not been receiving their desires yet. All they needed was to ask and they would receive. He wanted to give to them.

God wants us to have our desires more than we want to have them. When we receive from Him, He receives blessing because our joy is full. In John 15:11, Jesus said, "These things have I spoken unto you, that my joy might remain in you, and that your joy might be full." He was talking about two types of joy—*His* joy and *our* joy. His joy, the fruit of the Spirit, is inside us. We can stir it up any time we need to keep our joy full.

But God does not want us to only have our joy full because we have to keep tapping into his joy. He does not want us to always be in a situation like David was in 1 Samuel 30. Some Christians love God and delight in Him, but they have not learned how to receive the desires of their hearts. Their joy is full only because they stir up the joy of the Lord. Thank God that we can stir up the joy of the Lord in every situation and enjoy the Lord as our strength that will see us through. However, God wants us to have our joy full because we have received good things.

Yes, God wants us to rejoice because we are believing God for a car, a mate, a promotion, and are receiving these gifts from His hand. Stirring up His joy is really an emergency policy, a reserve for the times when Satan comes against us with affliction and persecution. It is something to see us through so we can say, "God has delivered me." But God desires that we be so blessed that we are full of joy because of His blessing. He wants us to be full of joy because He is prospering us and giving us the desires of our hearts.

We need to talk about stirring up the joy of the Lord on the inside of us and teach on how to be a happy, joyful Christian. We should encourage ourselves in the Lord and rejoice all the time. But it is not God's will that we should always have to stir up our joy. God wants us to be happy because good things have happened to us. He wants us to have a merry heart and a continual feast because of His blessings (Prov. 15:15). He likes to see us smile because His gifts have caused us to have merry hearts (Prov. 15:13).

A parent has joy when they see their child enjoy something. I have experienced joy by giving my daughter something she enjoys, and that is how God feels with us. Jesus introduced us to the Father and said that if we give good gifts to our children, how much more will he give us good things if we ask Him (Matt. 7:9–11). The Father enjoys giving to us. He wants our joy to be full, and that tells me that joy can be empty, a quarter full, or half full. If our joy is not full, we need to stir up the joy of the Lord. However, God wants us to reach a place where we receive the desires of our heart and our joy is full because we have what we are believing to receive from God. Our Father gets joy out of that.

The Old Testament shows how God delights in giving us the desires of our heart. Second Chronicles 8:1–6 says that Solomon first built the Lord's house, then his house, and afterward everything he desired. He took care of God's business and then walked in whatever he desired. Some generations later in 2 Chronicles 26:5, God made King Uzziah to prosper "as long as he sought the LORD." One of the ways God blessed him was to give him livestock, fields, and vineyards because he loved working with plants and animals (verse 10).

God wants us to be like the Jewish exiles who had returned from Babylonian captivity and, in Psalm 126:1–2, said, "when the LORD turned again the captivity of Zion, we were like them that dream. Then was our mouth filled with laughter, and our tongue with singing: then said they among the heathen, The LORD hath done great things for them." God wants our lives to be like a dream. He wants us to be laughing because of what He has done for us. And He wants the joy in our lives to attract the attention of the heathen so that they see how He has done good things for us.

Delight in the Lord Above All Else

The key to receiving the desires of our hearts is that we delight in God above all else. Hebrews 12:1 instructs us to lay aside every weight and the sin that so easily besets us. Many times we focus on laying aside our besetting sins, but hang on to a few weights—things that take His place in our lives. God has dealt with me about delighting in sports. I love sports, and at one time I put my interest in that ahead of my time in God's Word. I would get up, have my prayer time, and then jump on the internet or grab a newspaper to see what was going on in sports. After that, I would take some time for the Word. God showed me that I was delighting myself in sports more than Him, and that would not give me the desires of my heart.

We must ask ourselves what takes our time before God does? To watch three or four hours of television every day, but not have time for a relationship with God in prayer and the Word shows that are we delighting in our television programs. To spend large amounts of time in a dating relationship and not have time for God means that we are delighting in that person or that relationship. God has to come first. He will give us the desires of our heart, but he has to be our number one desire.

How do we delight ourselves in God? Isaiah 58:2 says:

> Yet they seek me daily, and delight to know my ways, as a nation that did righteousness, and forsook not the ordinance of their God: they ask of me the ordinances of justice; they take delight in approaching to God.

This verse teaches us to delight ourselves in knowing God's Word and in going to Him in prayer. We could restate it, "they delight to know my Word." We may have the habit of going to church and spending time in prayer and the Word. However, doing these things by habit does not mean that we look forward to them. We may actually look beyond them to what we will do afterwards. How many times do we come to church on Sunday with our focus on what is going to happen after the service? Do we come to prayer thinking, "I cannot wait until I get done with this," or to the Word, thinking, "I cannot wait until I get to my TV show"?

The psalmist says, "I was glad when they said unto me, let us go into the house of the LORD" (Psalm 122:1). We should delight in coming to God at church, in prayer, and in the Word. We should look forward to that *first*. This requires a shift, an adjustment in our lives. We may begin right, but our enjoyment of God's blessings can pull us away. God still means, "You shall have no other Gods before me" (Exod. 20:3). That car, that hobby, that man or woman could be another god.

Something is wrong when we look forward to something beyond our time with God. Colossians 3:4 teaches that Christ is our life. Romans 6:13 says that we should live our lives unto God, not unto other things. There is nothing wrong with other things when they are in their place. However, if they are out of place, they become weights that hinder our spiritual development. We need to delight in God first.

An important part of delighting ourselves in God is serving Him in ministry opportunities. It is giving ourselves to evangelism so we can see the kingdom of God expand. If we are part of the kingdom of God, we should be excited about what it is doing. If we do not give ourselves to God and His kingdom work, how can we believe Him for the desires of our heart? Faith is a vital part of receiving God's blessings, but it is not everything.

> If thou turn away thy foot from the sabbath, from doing thy pleasure on my holy day; and call the sabbath a delight, the holy of the LORD, honourable; and shalt honour him, not doing thine own ways, nor finding thine own pleasure, nor speaking thine own words: Then shalt thou delight thyself in the LORD; and I will cause thee to ride upon the high places of the earth, And feed thee with the heritage of Jacob thy father: for the mouth of the Lord hath spoken it.
>
> —Isaiah 58:13–14

Isaiah 58 teaches us how to walk in total prosperity. In verse 13, God, through the prophet Isaiah, corrected His people because they were not honoring the Sabbath as He had commanded them.

Instead of delighting in the Sabbath, they were doing things for their own pleasure. God called them to delight in Him. And He promised that when they did this, He would cause them "to ride upon the high places of the earth." They would be blessed above all people. And that sounds like prosperity.

God calls us to delight in Him—in His Word, in prayer, and in His work. This means we choose and enjoy His presence and will as the source of our joy. He excites us. He turns our light on! He is our number one hobby. God does not look only at our actions, He looks at our hearts to see if He is the treasure we value most. He wants us to pray to Him and praise Him with our *whole* heart.

If God is number one in our lives, He will bless us with the desires of our heart. However, if we desire things of the world above God it is really lust, an inordinate strong desire for something. We want things more than we want our relationship with God, and we turn them into our god. The love of money—craving it and chasing after it as our source of joy and the answer to all our problems—is the root of all evil. Or we may think that having someone as our marriage partner will make us happy. We may do what it takes to get that person, but we will not get the desire of our heart.

When we lust after people and things, we look at them as the answer to all our problems. We believe that they will give us joy and make us feel better. However, if we are not looking to *God* as the answer, we are not in position to receive the things we desire. God is not going to give us things when we are looking at them as our God. We need to take our strong desires and turn them toward God. When we do, we will enjoy His blessings.

The history of Israel gives us a great object lesson of this truth. Israel had lived in Egypt for 430 years, much of that time as slaves, and the heart's desire of the people was to leave Egypt and have their own land. God gave them a dream, a desire for Canaan, the Promised Land, "a land flowing with milk and honey" (Exod. 13:5). He could have taken the people of Israel out of Egypt and brought them into the land of Canaan in a very short time. Deuteronomy 1:2 says the journey to Kadeshbarnea, which was near the southern edge of Canaan, took just eleven days. However, He didn't.

Instead, God took time to do some important things to prepare His people to enter the land they desired. First, God gave Israel his laws. One of those laws was, "You shall have no other God before Me" (Exod. 20:3). Another was, "Love the LORD your God with all your heart and with all your soul and with all your might" (Deut. 6:5). God wanted His people to delight in Him. In addition to giving them His laws, He also directed them to build a tabernacle, a place where he could dwell among them.

Two years after Israel came out of Egypt, Moses sent twelve spies to explore the Promised Land. Ten of the twelve came back with a bad report, and the people cried and wept (Num. 13:1–14:1). They believed they would not be able to experience their dream, the desire of their heart. They were not in position to receive because they were not delighting in God, and He could not bring them into the land. As a result, they wandered in the wilderness for thirty-eight years, until the generation that doubted God had died. And during that time, God tested the people to see if they would obey his laws (Deut. 8:2).

The next generation showed that it would delight in God.

The people reached the place where *God* was everything and they would do whatever He said. They were completely in position and received their hearts' desires. They walked in the land, took Jericho, and defeated all the nations Satan had arrayed against them. Joshua 23:14 says that God fulfilled all His promises to them. Everything came to pass. What joy the people must have experienced as they watched what God was doing! As each tribe took possession of the land God had given them, they exclaimed, "Look what God has done."

We can be like the people of Israel who received the Promised Land, the desire of their hearts. We do not have to live in the wilderness, going in circles and just getting our needs met. While we need to learn God's laws, the most important thing is that we *delight* in Him. As we delight in God and His Word, we can come out of the wilderness and walk in the good land He has promised us. We can enjoy the desires of our hearts.

God has given us the key to the toy store of His blessings for us. It is delighting in Christ as our life, our source of joy. It is making the adjustment to place the highest value on our time in the Word, in prayer, and at His house. To delight in God is to enjoy Him as our everything, the reason we live. It is seeking first His kingdom, then we might enjoy all the desires of our hearts.

The following keys will enable us to receive the desires of our hearts:

- **Sell out to God**—Lay aside the weights that beset you and truly live your life for God. First Thessalonians 4:1 teaches us that we ought to please God more and more. Make pleasing God, as well as loving God, the center of your life.

- **Obey God's direction for your life**—When Abraham obeyed God and went to Canaan, God gave him his desire to have a son. What has God called you to do? Enter into God's will for your life.

- **Ask in faith**—When you come to God for whatever you need or desire, believe that you will receive the right thing. "He that cometh to God must believe that he is, and that he is a rewarder of them that diligently seek him" (Heb. 11:6). Faith is required.

- **Be patient**—Hebrews 6:12-15 tells us to follow the example of those "who through faith and patience inherit the promises" and identifies Abraham as one who obtained the promise of God's blessing. James 1:4 says, 'But let patience have her perfect work, that ye may be perfect and entire, wanting nothing." Get in position to receive the desires of your heart and you will enjoy delightful living.

Chapter 4

ENTERING INTO WELLNESS

And the LORD *heard the voice of your words,
when ye spake unto me; and the* Lord *said unto
me, I have heard the voice of the words of this
people, which they have spoken unto thee: they
have well said all that they have spoken. O that
there were such an heart in them, that they would
fear me, and keep all my commandments always,
that it might be well with them, and
with their children for ever!*
—Deuteronomy 5:28–29

WHEN GOD GAVE Israel the Ten Commandments, the people heard them and told Moses, "We will do all that you told us God wants us to do." In response to this, God spoke out of His heart: "O that there were such an heart in them, that they would fear me and keep all my commandments" (Deut. 5:29). However, God knew that the people of Israel did not have such a heart.

God wanted his people to keep his Word not for the sake of keeping it, but so they could enjoy the end result: "that it may be well with them." He revealed the intensity of this desire by introducing it with the interjection "O." And He has not changed. His desire today is the same as it was then. He wants it to be well with us, that we will prosper in every arena of life and have no lack.

Every person I know, whether they are saved or unsaved, wants it to be well with them. But this is the Most High God, the Almighty, the Creator of the Universe who is looking at our lives and saying, "O, that it would be well with them." He wants us to prosper in our marriage and family relationships and in our jobs. He loves us, and He wants everything we do to go well.

In Psalm 139:14 David expresses praise to God as his Creator who has made him fearfully and wonderfully. He rejoices because he is one of God's jewels, reverently and uniquely made, one of a kind. In verses 17–18, he exclaims, "How precious also are thy thoughts unto me, O God! how great is the sum of them! If I should count them, they are more in number than the sand."

God is thinking about you and me. He has us on His mind. He does not just think about us once a year. No, His thoughts about us are more in number than the sand on the seashore. In Matthew 10:29–31 Jesus says that not one sparrow falls to the ground apart from the Father's knowledge, and we are more valuable than many sparrows. He pays attention to us, and even knows the number of hairs on our heads.

When my wife and I were waiting for our daughter to be born, we wondered what she would look like. Now that she is here, I have looked at her countless times. She is so precious to me, and I know every detail of her face. I can tell if something is wrong. That is how God views you and me. He loves us abundantly, more than our minds can understand, and He is thinking about us all the time. He wants to bless us.

Psalm 115:11–12 addresses those who fear the Lord and says, "The Lord hath been mindful of us: he will bless us." It is no coincidence that these two phrases are together. God has you and me on his mind, and He will bless us. His thoughts toward us, His desires, are that we be blessed.

God repeats this in Jeremiah 29:11, "For I know the thoughts that I think toward you...thoughts of peace, and not of evil," thoughts to give you the future you hope for. Yes, God is thinking about you and me. He is thinking about blessing us so that it will be well with us. He greatly desires that we be able to look at our lives and say, it is well with me and my family. It is well with me and my body. It is well with me and my finances. It is well with me and my emotions. It is well with me and my job. It is well with me.

It is important that we understand what God said in Deuteronomy 5:29. He did not just say, "O, that it would be well with them." He said, "O that there were such an heart in them that they would fear me, and keep all my commandments." We will examine biblical teaching on the fear of the Lord—reverence and awe toward God—in chapter 7. In this chapter, however, we will learn how important it is to obey God if we want to enter into the place of wellness. God's Word has established how His kingdom works here on earth.

His plan is that we cooperate with Him and obey Him. We must keep his commandments to fully experience God's desire for it to be well with us.

The Priority of Pleasing God

The story of Ruth presents the priority of pleasing God as an important key to wellness. Ruth was a Moabite woman who married one of the sons of Elimelech and Naomi, an Israelite couple who had left their home in Bethlehem to live in Moab. Elimelech died, as did both his sons, and Naomi decided to return to Bethlehem. She told Ruth and her sister-in-law, Orpah, to go back to their homes in Moab, and Orpah did. However, Ruth did something extraordinary. She told her mother-in-law, "I am going with you. I am going to die where you die. I am going to serve your God" (author's paraphrase). She chose to go with her mother-in-law to another country where she would be a stranger.

Ruth was a selfless individual, a virtuous, hardworking woman who was determined to be a blessing to Naomi. When they got to Bethlehem, she went out into the fields and worked from morning to evening so they could have something to eat. She became known for her life of service for her mother-in-law. And this is the point at which Ruth 3:1 introduces God's plan to bless Ruth: "Then Naomi her mother in law said unto her, My daughter, shall I not seek rest for thee, that it may be well with thee?"

The word "rest" means quiet, a settled spot or a home. At this time it was commonly believed that a woman who did not have a husband really was incomplete; therefore, it was not well with her. Naomi recognized that Ruth had left her family, her home, and, it would seem, the possibility of having a home of her own. In essence Naomi was asking, "Should not I be seeking a husband for you so you can have a home?" However, Ruth was not seeking for rest herself. Instead, she was focused on serving and being a blessing. In the words of Romans 12:11, she was "Not slothful in business; fervent in spirit; serving the Lord."

Yes, Ruth had her priorities right, and she modeled how single believers should live today. A single person who wants to receive the person of God's choosing needs to be the person God wants him to be. Proverbs 31:10 asks, "Who can find a virtuous woman?" The word "find" means who can attain, who can get hold of a virtuous woman. And the answer is, not any bozo. The husband of the virtuous woman sat among the elders (Prov. 31:23). He was an accomplished man.

Ruth was not even thinking about her own life when Naomi said, "And now is not Boaz of our kindred, with whose maidens thou wast? Behold, he winnoweth barley to night in the threshingfloor" (Ruth 3:2). She gave Ruth instructions on how to communicate to Boaz that he could find someone to marry her or he could marry her himself. And, of course, she did become the wife of this "mighty man of wealth" (Ruth 2:1). This was not a coincidence. God set it up. Ruth 2 tells how it just so happened that Ruth went to the field of Boaz. It just so happened that he came to visit the field that day and saw her. God brought Boaz into her life so that it would be well with her.

What put Ruth in position to receive this blessing from God? Why do we read about her today, more than three thousand years later? She made pleasing God her priority. First

Corinthians 7:32 identifies this key to wellness when it speaks about the single person who cares for the things of God." As we focus on this priority, whether we are single or married, we will receive what we desire from God. Our obedience will bring us to the place of wellness.

The longer I am in God's Word, the simpler the things of His kingdom are. If we are not getting a certain result in our lives, it is because we are not doing something. Jesus said, "Seek ye first the Kingdom of God and his righteousness, and all these things will be added unto you" (Matt. 6:33). If things are not being added to us, we must not be obeying this verse. The same principle holds for Psalm 37:4, which we discussed in chapter 3. If we do not have the desires of our hearts, we must not be delighting ourselves in the Lord.

Jesus said, "The Son of man came not to be ministered unto, but to minister" (Mark 10:45). He did not come for people to serve him, but to serve people. Should not we follow His example? God wants us to serve in the church. He wants us to do what He said because then it would be well with us. God wants us to do what is right. First Peter 2:18 teaches: "Servants, be subject to your masters...not only to the good and gentle, but also to the froward." He tells us to relate to them as He says regardless of how they treat us. As Jesus says in Matthew 5:44, we are to "Bless them that curse you...and pray for them which despitefully use you."

That It May Be Well Between Husband and Wife

The phrase "that it may be well with you," speaks of much more than money and material possessions. Those things do not mean anything if our marriage relationships are not right. We have to understand this and give honor to each other as husband and wife. This key of honor fore each other is important if we are to experience wellness in the marriage bond. God created marriage, and we need to follow His plans for it. It is essential that we fear God and obey Him in this area of life.

In 1 Peter 3:1–7, the apostle Peter showed how it can be right in our homes. In verse 1, he instructed wives to do what is right by their husbands, whether they obey the Word of God or not. Wives are to submit to their husbands and truly reverence and respect them. God expects wives to make internal changes so that they truly reverence their husbands and not just act like it. It is wrong for a wife to use the excuse that she would submit if her husband would do this or that. No matter whom a woman marries, he will not be perfect. God says that she should submit and show reverence because that is what He tells her to do.

Peter continued his teaching about the marriage relationship with instructions to husbands in verse 7:

> Likewise, ye husbands, dwell with them according to knowledge, giving honour unto the wife, as unto the weaker vessel, and as being heirs together of the grace of life; that your prayers be not hindered.

Husbands, just like their wives, are to do what God says no matter how their mate treats them. *The Bible in Basic English* renders verse 7, "Give thought to your way of life with your wife."[1] Husbands are to think about how they live with their wives. They are to dwell with their wives, and not live under separate roofs or take separate vacations. A husband and wife are one.

God tells husbands to provide for their wives and honor them. The word "honor" means to value. It means money paid, esteem of the highest degree. Most men honor and esteem their mothers, but they must be careful to hold their wives in an even higher place of honor. They must give honor to the position of their wives, even if they think their wives do not deserve honor. To show honor, they must make a heart adjustment in the way they view their wives. They must see their wives as queens. When they do this, it will manifest itself in their actions wherever they are, at home or in public.

Prayer is another key to wellness. We need to come to God in prayer so He can make it well with us. As we noted in chapter 1, Jesus said, "What things soever ye desire, when ye pray, believe that ye receive them, and ye shall have them" (Mark 11:24). And in John 15:7 He added, "If ye abide in me, and my words abide in you, ye shall ask what ye will, and it shall be done unto you." We need to come boldly to the throne of grace and obtain mercy and find grace to help in time of need (Heb. 4:16). As we pray fervently, tremendous power will be made available in our lives.

However, if husbands do not treat their wives right, their prayers will be hindered. God will cover up His ears, and their prayers will be cut off. It cannot be well with us if God is not hearing our prayers. And it cannot be well with husbands if they are mistreating their wives. A husband will not be happy if he makes his wife unhappy, and God will not bless him.

We understand that we can pray, believe and receive. We understand grace and the precious truth that Jesus has already provided everything we need. But we also need to walk in holiness and obedience. We cannot live any old way and then believe and receive and have God's blessings. Yes, husbands need to give honor to their wives. They need to treat their wives the way God wants them to treat her, so they can receive from him and it will be well with them.

In Malachi 2:11–14 God confronted the people of Judah for their unfaithfulness to Him. He said that He would cut off the man who broke his covenant with Him, and He would not receive the offerings he brought to the altar. God has been witness between you and your wife. He has seen how you treated your wife. When we bring our offerings to God, we expect to receive His blessing, the anointing to prosper, that it may be well with us. However husbands and wives cannot treat each other any old way and expect to receive God's blessing. They have to treat each other as God has commanded.

When a man marries his wife, it means that he is committing himself to please her. This is much more that appeasing her and doing just enough to keep her happy. He should learn what his wife wants from him, and then do it, even if he does not feel like it. In the Mosaic law, Deuteronomy 24:5 instructed a new husband to take the first year after his marriage to cheer up his wife. The phrase "cheer up" means to brighten up, to make gleeful. The husband's job is to bring pleasure to his wife (1 Cor. 7:33), to cause her to be ravished with love.

The husband needs to plan how he can meet his wife's need

for affection. This need may take different forms, but typically it involves quality time. It may be hugging her without sexual intentions, or holding her hand in public. One way a husband can please his wife is by planning a date with her. She wants to feel like a princess who is wooed by her knight in shining armor. And, as 1 Corinthians 7:3 says, the husband and the wife are to render to each other due benevolence, to minister to the sexual needs they each have. The word "due" means something owed. It is a financial term, and one translation renders it, the debt.

It is very important that the husband and wife obey the teaching of God's Word in their sexual relationship. When they were married, they committed themselves to care for the sexual needs of each other all the days of their lives. Love gives, and the husband and wife are to walk in love toward each other. Their focus should be on pleasing each other so that they are both ravished with love. First Corinthians 7:5 warns the husband and wife that they should not defraud each other. There should be no unmet needs. If they do not care for the sexual needs of each other, they are placing themselves in the temptation zone and make themselves vulnerable to extra-marital affairs.

The husband and wife are to speak to each other with honor, as if they were a king and a queen. Colossians 3:19 tells husbands not to be bitter against their wives. As the Amplified translation says, "Do not be harsh with them." And Ephesians 5:33 instructs wives to reverence their husbands. When a husband and wife hurl angry words at each other, nobody is listening. No one is surely trying to gain an understanding. They have violated James 1:19, "Wherefore, my beloved brethren, let every man be swift to hear, slow to speak, slow to wrath."

When a husband and wife honor each other as royalty, they will refrain from speaking harmful words to each other. When they are tempted to be angry, they must learn to listen and learn to be slow to wrath. They must practice love, which does not keep track of the evil done to it. The Bible teaches us to forgive each other and walk in love with one another as He walks in love with us (Eph. 4:32–5:2). Words are the most powerful things we possess. They can tear a person down or build a person up (Eph. 4:29). God calls husbands and wives to build each other up.

Ephesians 5:25 says, "Husbands, love your wives, even as Christ also loved the church, and gave himself for it." On the other side, Ephesians 5:22 says, "Wives, submit yourselves unto your own husbands, as unto the Lord." This is what God expects of husbands and wives, so that they will receive His anointing and all will be well. When husbands and wives honor each other in this way, they bless each other. Give and it shall be given to you (Luke 6:38) is not just a financial principle. It is also a marriage principle that husbands and wives must practice.

That It May Be Well Between Children and Parents

Another key to wellness is the way we treat our parents. Ephesians 6:2–3 says that it will be well with us if we honor them. This is talking not only to young children, but to adults as well. When God gave this "first commandment with promise," he was talking to adults. Although we as adults do not have to obey our parents any more, we are clearly instructed to honor them. This means that we care for them to the best of our ability when they are in their later years. If they are wrong about something, we are to approach them with respect and express our concern. If they have failed us, we are to reverence their position.

Ephesians 6:4 introduces yet another key to wellness when it tells fathers, "Provoke not your children to wrath." Colossians 3:21 says almost the same thing and adds, "lest they be discouraged." The Amplified translation renders this phrase, "Do not break their spirits." We discourage our children when we are not consistent with them. Often we communicate that an activity is OK one minute, but it is not just a few minutes later. We also fail them when we do not give them our time and instead communicate the idea that they are just a problem. It will not be well with us when we do not care for the little jewels God has entrusted to us.

God specifically instructs fathers to bring up their children "in the nurture and admonition of the Lord" (Eph. 6:4). Fathers are responsible to provide for the spiritual development of their children. They are to teach their children the Word of God in the morning, at night, and as they go throughout the day (Deut. 6:7). And they are to love on them and be there for them. Real men serve God so that they can prosper in their family relationships.

The Bible teaches the importance of disciplining our children. Proverbs 23:13–14 says, "Withhold not correction from the child. If you beatest him with the rod, he shall not die. You will save his soul from hell." And Proverbs 13:24 adds, "If you do not discipline him, you do not love him." Fathers have to be about the business of raising mighty seed, wise children who will make them glad (Proverbs 10:1).

What can we do so that it will be well with us? In chapter 1, we saw how Job 36:11 described the righteous, "If they obey and serve him, they shall spend their days in prosperity, and their years in pleasures." Did you notice the *if*: if they obey, if they serve? And Psalm 35:27 reminds us that God takes pleasure in the prosperity of his servant. He enjoys seeing us, his sons and daughters, prosper. We serve a God who loves us and wants it to be well with us. The master key is that we fear Him and keep all His commandments.

Chapter 5

FRUITFUL, PROSPEROUS LIVING

Ye have not chosen me, but I have chosen you, and
ordained you, that ye should go and bring forth
fruit, and that your fruit should remain:
that whatsoever ye shall ask of the Father
in my name, he may give it you.
—John 15:16

WE DID NOT choose God. Rather, He chose us. When Jesus taught this important truth to His disciples the night before He died, He also told them that He had ordained them to go and bring forth fruit. The word "ordained" means to place to a point, to set forth. Just like the disciples, Jesus selected you and placed you. He appointed you and set you forth. H gave you an assignment to go and bring forth fruit.

God's will is that every believer bring forth fruit. This is not just for pastors or people who have been in the church for many years. God wants every follower of Christ to produce fruit because our fruitfulness determines our prosperity. This is very important to God. And if we love the Lord our God with all our heart, all our soul and all our might, we will be interested in the things that are important to Him.

Jesus said that our fruit should remain, that "whatsoever" we ask of the Father in His name He may give it to us. Whatsoever includes everything—health, wealth, victory, protection, peace in our hearts, whatever we desire from God. The will of God is that we be able to come into his presence boldly, with confidence, and ask for whatsoever we desire from him.

In John 15:7 Jesus said, "If ye abide in me, and my words abide in you, ye shall ask what ye will, and it shall be done unto you." If we meet these criteria we can come to Him and ask for whatever we will. The word "will" means to determine, to delight in. It means that Jesus has given us a blank check. Of course, we must ask for things according to His will, as 1 John 5:14 teaches. It is obvious that we cannot come to God and ask for our neighbor's wife. Jesus is talking about things that are according to His will, and they are in the bank account of His riches and glory.

It is as though Jesus is saying, "I have given you a blank check. You fill it out and I will go ahead and cash the check." That is good news! The government cannot say that, and neither can a family member. However, God can say, "Ask me for whatever you want, whatever you desire. Ask for whatever you need to be whole, and I will give it to you." Oh, that is good news! We can ask what we will and it shall be done.

The Bible teaches us in 2 Peter 1:3 that God has given us who are born again "all things that pertain unto life and godliness." He has given us exceeding great and precious promises so we can partake of all those blessings. All we need to do is get a hold of the promises and learn what His will is. If we can find it in His Word, we can come to Him and He will give it to us.

> And in that day ye shall ask me nothing. Verily, verily, I say unto you, Whatsoever ye shall ask the Father in my name, he will give it you. Hitherto have ye asked nothing in my name: ask, and ye shall receive, that your joy may be full.
> —John 16:23–24

This is one of God's great and precious promises for "that day," the day we live in now since Christ's death and resurrection. Jesus emphasized that we need to pay attention to this promise by saying "verily, verily"—truly, truly. Jesus, who declared, "I am the Truth," was about to say something that would typically be hard to believe if He had not said it. It would seem too good to be true if we did not know how good our God is.

Jesus promised that that the Father would give us whatsoever we ask in His name. Whatsoever means whatever need we have. The apostle Paul talked about this in Romans 8:32, where it says that if God "spared not his own son, but delivered him up for us all, how shall he not with him also freely give us all things?" God gave us Jesus, so what can compare to Him? If someone gives his friend a million dollars, what is another five? Yes, God gave us Jesus. Of course he will give us protection and healing. Of course he will give us wealth and a prosperous family. Of course he will give us victory and anything we desire in this life. He gave us Jesus and demonstrated the fact that it is His good will to give us whatever we need so we can have prosperity and eternal life.

As we stated in chapter 3, God wants our joy to be full. He is not talking about His joy within us, but about our joy. He gave us His joy when we received Christ as Lord, but we also have our joy. God is actually interested in us being emotionally prosperous, happy, well-off, and enjoying life. He tells us to ask what you will and He will give it to you so your joy will be filled up. This promise in not limited to requests for spiritual things. God does care about our lives today, and He wants us to prosper. He wants us to eat the good of the land and enjoy life today, as well as in the days and ages to come.

In Mark 11:24 Jesus said, "Therefore I say unto you, What things soever ye desire, when ye pray, believe that ye receive them, and ye shall have them." We can ask God for the things His Word promises, whatever we desire. He is interested not only in meeting our needs, but also in bringing us to a place where our desires are met.

We Are Overcomers

As we begin to step in and receive the promises of God, we will face opposition from the enemy. However, God has prepared victory for us. The Bible teaches that we are kings and priests under God, and this is true now, not just when we get to heaven. As priests, we must live holy lives, for without holiness no man will see the Lord (Heb. 12:14). As kings, we reign. Romans 5:17 says that all who have received Jesus will reign in life, as the Amplified Bible says, as kings. God's will is that we reign in this life, that we prosper and dominate instead of being dominated by things such as sickness and poverty.

Second Corinthians 2:14 says, "Thanks be unto God, which always causeth us to triumph." First Corinthians 15:57 adds, "Thanks be to God, which giveth us the victory." We have been called to live victorious lives. We may know this, but we forget about it when we are in the middle of the battle. When we are in the trenches, we forget that we are victorious. We forget about dominating and start thinking about merely surviving. We have been given enough equipment to not only make it, but to also push back the gates of hell and be victorious here on Earth. We are world overcomers, more than conquerors. We are champions in the realm of the spirit.

We have authority in the name of Jesus. When we use the name of Jesus, the anointing of God comes, and there is no Goliath we cannot knock down. There is no mountain that cannot be moved, no Red Sea that cannot be parted. There is no obstacle that we cannot overcome by the blood of the Lamb and the Word of God. God did not promise we would not have trouble in this life, but He did promise that we will win. The good fight of faith is a fight, but God guarantees that we will win. We must not get discouraged or give up. If we just stay in the ring and keep on believing God as we throw punches at the enemy, it will not be long before he falls down.

God has made us a special breed of people. We walk on this earth as human divine, children of God, heirs of God, joint heirs with Jesus Christ. We are supermen and superwomen in the realm of the Spirit. We can call on the power of God whenever we need it and cause it to manifest in a situation.

It is time that we started using what we have. We must

choose to take what we are, be what we are, use what God has given us and knock the enemy out. We are overcomers and champions. When we walk into the arena, we know we are going to win. Even if we fall down, we know that we are going to win in the end. We will win in Jesus' name because of who we are and whom we serve. We must not give up. There is no place for discouragement in the body of Christ.

Instead, we need to do our victory dance ahead of time. When a football player crosses into the end zone, he often does a little dance. Sometimes a player gets in trouble because he starts dancing a few yards before he is in the end zone. But that is a good thing in our life as believers. It is a good thing to break out with a victory dance while we are walking on the water, before we reach our goal. Let's thank God for the victory and tell the devil, "Ha-ha, you lost again."

Romans 16:20 promises, "And the God of peace shall bruise Satan under your feet shortly." He is going to pick up our feet and stomp them on Satan's head, and He is going to do it shortly. This does not mean five years from now; it could be a minute from now, tomorrow, or next week. It could be this instant. God wants to make us Satan-stomping weapons in this life. We do not need to feel like victims because we have the Word, the anointing, the name of Jesus, the blood. We can know we are victors.

As Nehemiah 8:10 says, "The joy of the Lord is our strength." When we are in the midst of the battle, Satan tries to steal our joy by attacking us in our thought life. He sends us thoughts about our situation and reminds us how long we have been fighting. His goal is to plant thoughts of doubt and discouragement that we will meditate on until they produce the fruit of fear in our lives. We have to stop him at the door, and, as 2 Corinthians 10:5 says, bring every thought into the captivity of Christ. Philippians 4:8 teaches us to think only those things that are true, honest, just, pure, lovely, and of good report.

We have to monitor what we think about during this time of trouble. We should think such things as, "Thanks be to God who always causes me to triumph; I am more than a conqueror" (Rom. 8:37); "This is the victory that overcometh the world, even [my] faith" (1 John 5:4) When we stand in faith and speak the Word of God, our mountains will move. When Satan sends his thoughts our way, we can say, "I rebuke that in the authority of Jesus." Then we can encourage ourselves by saying what God says about our struggles. Our joy level will stay up and our joy will see us through.

David encouraged himself in the Lord when he was in great distress in I Samuel 30:6, and we can too. But we have to make a choice. We can give up and get depressed, or we can choose to walk in victory. We may face difficult situations that seem unique to us, but there is no problem that God cannot handle. His arm is not short. The issue is not our problems, but how we respond. God told Joshua, "Be strong and of a good courage" (Josh. 1:6) And the apostle Paul encouraged us, "Be strong in the Lord, and in the power of his might" (Eph. 6:10).

Whatsoever Means Whatsoever

An important part of victorious living is God's promise that we receive whatsoever we desire (John 16:23). Whatsoever means whatsoever. Psalm 37:4 says, "Delight thyself also in the Lord: and he shall give thee the desires of thine heart." God knows the very hairs on our heads, and we can be sure that He knows the very details of our desires too. He wants to give them to us because He wants us to enjoy this life. First Timothy 6:17 teaches us that God gives us richly all things to enjoy. These are promises of prosperity, which is much greater than money. These promises describe wholeness.

As we saw in chapter 3, Ecclesiastes 5:18–20 tells how good and beautiful it is to see a man of God enjoy the good of all his labor and partake of his riches and wealth. It reveals the goodness of God's heart toward us. And Job 22:24–26 encourages us to delight in God and promises gold as the dust and plenty of silver. We are talking about more than enough gold to pay our bills. This is overflow, and it is the way God thinks.

Many times we let the world dictate how we think. However, even though we are in the world, we are not of it. We may be citizens of a nation here on earth, but we are most importantly citizens of the Kingdom of God. It is therefore important that we do some Kingdom thinking. God wants to get the gospel message out, and we have to start believing what He said to accomplish this in the financial arena. If He said gold as the dust, we must believe Him for that. If He said good measure, pressed down and shaken together, running over (Luke 6:38), we must believe Him for that. God wants to bless us to be a blessing, but He also wants to bless us because He wants us to enjoy His blessings. This is why He says *whatsoever*, whatever you want.

If my wife or daughter asks me for something, I'll say, "Whatever you want, whatever is in my ability." I love them and I want to give to them. When my daughter was very young, she found a toy bear in a store at the mall. She picked it up, put it down, walked away, and then came back and picked it up again. The third time she did this, she looked at me, and yes, I bought it for her because I love her. As Jesus taught in Luke 11:11–13, if we, as natural parents, love our children so much that we give them gifts, how much more does our heavenly Father love us and want to give to us?

Second Corinthians 9:11 shows the will of God for our lives: "Being enriched in every thing..." In the preceding verses, Paul was encouraging the church to give an offering. He talked about sowing and reaping and said that when we sow, God's grace will come into our lives. And in verse 11 he said that God's grace will bring us to the place where we are enriched. The Greek word for "enriched" means to be made wealthy. The will of God is that we be made wealthy *in every thing*.

Psalm 128 talks about the man who fears God and says that it will be well with him. The New Living translation renders this, "how rich your life." And that is what God wants. He does not just want us to be rich financially. He wants us to have a rich life, to be enriched in everything. God takes pleasure in the prosperity we enjoy as His children, just as a parent enjoys seeing his child prosper.

God wants us to be blessed and enriched in every arena of life—in our marriages, our health, in victories, in protection, with the mighty seed of wonderful children, and in material wealth. This is why He says that whatever you need, whatever you desire He will give it to you. And Job 36:11 promises that if we obey and serve him, we will spend our days in prosperity and our years in pleasures.

When God created this planet for us He made it with all of the things we have and use today. He provided it for us so we could enjoy life. When sin entered the world, it brought difficulties, suffering, and death into our lives. God's answer to this was the gift of salvation through His Son Jesus Christ, and today we preach the gospel—the good news—about this. We use the gold, the money God has provided in the earth to help do this. But there was no gospel to be preached when God made the earth. He gave us the riches of this world for us to enjoy, both in the beginning and today. And when we get to heaven, we will find that the streets are made of gold.

Ordained to Bring Forth Fruit

We serve a good God, a wonderful Father who wants us to prosper and be blessed. He has provided abundantly for us and has told us how to receive all that He has promised. This truth is an important part of Jesus' teaching in John 15:16. But this scripture points us to another important part of God's will with the phrase "that ye should go and bring forth fruit."

God is very interested in seeing us bring forth fruit—yes, much fruit—for Him. We see this in the emphasis Jesus put on fruit in John 15. He said:

> Every branch in me that beareth not fruit he taketh away: and every branch that beareth fruit, he purgeth it, that it may bring forth more fruit...Abide in me, and I in you. As the branch cannot bear fruit of itself, except it abide in the vine; no more can ye, except ye abide in me. I am the vine, ye are the branches: He that abideth in me, and I in him, the same bringeth forth much fruit...Herein is my Father glorified, that ye bear much fruit..."
>
> —John 15:2, 4–5, 8

What is fruit? God refers to good works and the harvest of wealth as fruit. But He is most interested in seeing us produce the fruit of winning souls. Daniel 12:3 says that those who turn many to righteousness shall shine as the stars. Proverbs 11:30 teaches us, "He that winneth souls is wise." The heart of God, His desire, is souls. That is what He is all about. He sent His Son to die for our sins and rise again so that all people could have the opportunity to come into His family. If we love the Lord our God with all our heart and all our soul and all our might, we are going to be interested in winning souls above all other things.

James 5:7 describes God as the husbandman who is waiting for the precious fruit of the earth. He is waiting and waiting for the harvest of lost souls to come into the Kingdom of God. God's heart is to reach every individual on this earth. Second Peter 3:9 says it is His will that all men be saved. This is why Jesus told us, "Go ye into all the world, and preach the gospel" (Mark 16:15). God wants us to produce fruit by winning souls.

But winning souls is only part of God's will for us. He also wants our fruit to remain. We may go out and win someone to Christ, but sometimes that is all that we do with that person. It is important that we help to consolidate and establish new believers in their relationship with Christ. We need to win the lost *and* consolidate the found.

The Book of Acts describes the pattern of the apostle Paul's ministry as going to a city, preaching the word, leading a group of people to faith in Christ, and moving on to another city. After a while, however, he would come back to the city and make sure the people who had been saved were established in the faith. The church today needs to learn from this. We are responsible to consolidate new Christians and help them become established in the faith, as Jesus taught in the Great Commission:

> All power is given unto me in heaven and in earth. Go ye therefore, and teach all nations, baptizing them in the name of the Father, and of the Son, and of the Holy Ghost: Teaching them to observe all things whatsoever I have commanded you.
>
> —Matthew 28:18–20

God wants us to win the lost and also help new believers become established in the Body of Christ. We are to make disciples of all nations and teach them the things God has taught us. And we are to baptize new followers of Christ, thus practicing a key to consolidating people.

How do we know that our fruit remains? The phrase "fruit that remains" refers to someone who has been born again and established in the faith and is now producing for God. We must ask ourselves the question, "Who am I helping to disciple?" Every pastor needs people who can help establish young believers. Hebrews 10:25 says that we come together as a church so that we can exhort one another, to help others develop in their relationship with God.

God's promise to give us whatsoever we ask of Him comes after the first half of John 15:16. We cannot expect God to prosper us in every arena of life just because we throw some money in the offering bucket or come to Him in prayer. We must also do our part to help rescue the millions who are going to hell. We will not prosper in this life if we do not produce fruit. However, when we produce for God, He will produce for us.

If we do not bring forth fruit and our fruit does not remain, we do not qualify for the second half of John 15:16. We cannot come and ask for "whatsoever" if we are not obeying God and loving Him with all that we are. We cannot come to God in confidence because our conscience is not right with Him. Perhaps we have worked with someone fifteen years and have never told that person about Jesus. Even if we work around other Christians and are rarely with someone who is lost, we still meet people who need Christ when we go to the grocery store or the mall. They are walking by us all the time.

We may have any number of excuses for why we do not witness to those who do not know Christ. However, God will not accept them. If we say that we don't know how, we have failed to take advantage of training that is available to us. If we say that we are afraid, we cannot escape the promise of 2 Timothy 1:7, "For God hath not given us the spirit of fear; but of power, and of love, and of a sound mind." And if we are concerned about what people will think about us, we need to ask ourselves why that is true. Our concern should be to do what God told us to do. The only thing that matters is what God says.

It is inexcusable to receive so much Word and never share it. We should witness for Christ on a very consistent basis, to our neighbors and to the people who sit next to us on an airplane. In Matthew 9:37, Jesus says, "The harvest truly is plenteous, but the laborers are few." Yes, the harvest is here. The world is ripe for the picking.

In John 4:34, after He had just finished winning a woman to the Kingdom, Jesus told His disciples:

> My meat is to do the will of him that sent me, and to finish
> his work. Say not ye, There are yet four months, and then
> cometh harvest? behold, I say unto you, Lift up your eyes,
> and look on the fields; for they are white already to harvest.
> And he that reapeth receiveth wages.
>
> —John 4:34–36

Jesus promised that "he that reapeth receiveth wages." The word "wages" means pay for service, and God pays us well when we work for Him. This is why we see people in ministry receive rich blessings from God. They are going to the field and reaping souls, and they qualify to prosper in every arena of life. We see this principle at work in the life of Abraham. His assignment was different than ours, but he did what God told him to do. He followed God's call to the land of Canaan, and he was blessed in all things. If Abraham had not obeyed God, he never would have had a son. None of the promises would have come to pass because they all were dependent on his obedience to God.

We can produce fruit by giving, praying for others, or serving in ministries inside the church. This will help the kingdom of God expand indirectly. But the main way of doing this is to win souls and make disciples. When Jesus said to go into all the world and preach the gospel, he intended it for every believer. We are to be on the front lines, to battle the enemy by witnessing for Christ. Ephesians 4:11–12 says that Christ gave ministry gifts to the church for the perfecting and training of the saints, so they can go and do the work of the ministry. He has provided training so that we can go out and fight in the battle, and it is so important that each of us receive this training and then go out to battle.

People should know that they are going to hear about Jesus when they talk to us. This is so important because people are going to hell every day. If I clap my hands four or five times, a soul is slipping into hell every time I clap. That shows how serious this is. We cannot just sit by and allow people God has put within our reach slip away without hearing the gospel from us.

Our Fruitfulness Determines Our Prosperity

Our fruitfulness determines our prosperity. When we produce fruit for God, He produces fruit for us. We cannot come down hard on the prosperity side but light on the fruitfulness side. We have to be true to the Word, which teaches that if we produce fruit God will give us whatsoever we ask. God says that if you bring people into His family and you make Him rich, He will make you rich.

In John 14:12–13, Jesus said, "Verily, verily, I say unto you, He that believeth on me, the works that I do shall he do also; and greater works than these shall he do; because I go unto my Father. And whatsoever ye shall ask in my name, that will I do." Jesus was teaching that all who believe on Him will do His works. His primary work was winning the lost and helping establish those who had been found. However, He also gave of Himself to others and ministered healing and deliverance. Second Timothy 3:16–17 says that all Scripture, the Word, was given to us so we God could be perfect, thoroughly furnished unto all the good works Jesus did.

Jesus made an important connection between verses 12 and

13. He said that He was going to His Father, and He would see to it Himself that all who believed in Him and did His works would receive whatsoever they asked in His name. In other words, He made a works-prosperity connection, a fruitfulness-prosperity connection.

Fruitfulness grows out of our faith in God. However, we also need to practice holiness and just do what He says. In Matthew 6:33, Jesus said, "But seek ye first the Kingdom of God, and his righteousness; and all these things shall be added unto you." The Amplified Version renders this verse, "But seek (aim at and strive after) first of all His Kingdom and His righteousness (His way of doing and being right)." As we seek God's kingdom and his way of doing things, He will add rich blessings to our lives.

When we seek God's kingdom, we give ourselves to help expand it. Jesus is building His church, and in Matthew 16:18 He said, "The gates of hell will not prevail against it." As Jesus works through His church, the kingdom of God is growing. In Colossians 4:11 the apostle Paul noted that he had fellow workers who were serving with him in the ministry of extending the kingdom of God. Today, God calls us to help the Kingdom increase by winning souls. We should think about souls more than we think about money. Our fruitfulness will determine our prosperity, so we need to bring forth fruit.

We serve a good God, who wants to make us fruitful and prosperous. If we have prayed and have not received what we asked, we need to examine our lives to see if we have been fully obedient to God's Word.

And it shall come to pass, if thou shalt hearken diligently unto the voice of the LORD thy God, to observe and to do all his commandments which I command thee this day, that the LORD thy God will set thee on high above all nations of the earth.

—Deuteronomy 28:1

As New Testament believers, we are not required to keep all the commandments the people of Israel had under the old covenant. For example, we do not have to sacrifice sheep and goats to God. However, we are still required to obey commandments such as Leviticus 19:18, "Thou shalt love thy neighbor as thyself." As we do all God's commandments, He will cause us to be blessed above all people. In John 14:21, Jesus promised, "He that hath my commandments, and keepeth them, he it is that loveth me: and he that loveth me shall be loved of my Father, and I will love him, will manifest myself to him."

After Jesus rose from the dead, He gave us the command to go and preach and disciple. This is the greatest interest of His heart, and we are responsible to fulfill it. If we love the Lord our God with all our heart, all our soul, and all our might, it will become our greatest interest too. And because we love Him with all our might, we will do what is necessary to obey Him. We will look beyond ourselves and see how the people around us need Jesus. And we will pray that God will open a door of utterance so that we can minister the gospel to them.

Jesus spoke a very strong message to us in Luke 6:46–49:

And why call ye me, Lord, Lord, and do not the things which I say? Whosoever cometh to me, and heareth my sayings, and doeth them, I will shew you to whom he is like: He is like a man which built an house [the house of his life, his prosperity] and digged deep, and laid the foundation on a rock: and when the flood arose, the stream beat vehemently upon that house, and could not shake it: for it was founded upon a rock. But he that heareth, and doeth not, is like a man that without a foundation built an house upon the earth; against which the stream did beat vehemently, and immediately it fell; and the ruin of that house was great."

These verses call us to truly honor Jesus as Lord by hearing His Word and doing it. As we obey God, we will bring forth fruit that remains. We will notice those who are lost and act on the fact that the blood of Jesus was shed not only for us, but for them too. We will share the gospel with them, recognizing that God has called both us *and* them. It is God's will that we prosper and also that those who are lost will trust in Christ and receive blessing and prosperity from Him. As we bring forth fruit for God, we will find that He will give us whatsoever we ask of him.

Chapter 6

STIRRING UP THE JOY
OF THE LORD

*So after he had washed their feet and had taken his
garments and was set down again, he said unto
them, Know ye what I have done to you? Ye call me
Master and Lord: and ye say well; for so I am.
If I then, your Lord and Master, have washed your
feet; you also ought to wash one another's feet.
For I have given you an example, that ye should do
as I have done to you. Verily, verily, I say unto you,
The servant is not greater than his lord; neither
he that is sent greater than he that sent him. If ye
know these things, happy are ye if you do them.*
—John 13:12–17

AFTER JESUS AND His twelve disciples finished
partaking of what is commonly called the Last
Supper, Jesus got up, exchanged His garments for a towel

and proceeded to wash His disciples' feet. When He had done this, He taught them about what He had done. "You call me your master and you call me your Lord," He said (author's paraphrase). "If I, your master, have knelt down and washed your feet, you also ought to wash one another's feet."

Jesus was not saying that we should have foot washing services, although there is nothing wrong with having a foot washing service. He was actually talking about something deeper than that. By washing His disciples' feet he was *serving* them, doing something for their benefit. After walking on the dusty roads of Jerusalem that day, their feet were dirty and needed to be washed. If Jesus, their master and Lord, was willing to serve them, surely they should be willing to serve one another.

The mentality of this world is that we need to reach a place of status so people will serve us. Jesus, however, said just the opposite in Matthew 20:26–28. Whoever wants to be the greatest, He taught, should be the servant. The person who is greatest in the kingdom of God is the person who is a servant. Describing Himself, Jesus declared, "The Son of man came not to be ministered unto, but to minister." He did not come to have people take care of Him, but to take care of people.

Jesus is the King of Kings. Naturally speaking, we would have expected God to send Him to earth with an invitation for all the people of the world to come together at the largest reception ever. Jesus should have received every kind of expensive gift and people should have bowed down before Him for weeks, caring for His every need. Yet that is not how God sent Him. Instead, the Father sent Him to a woman who was a virgin. At the time of His birth, she and her husband could find no room in the inn, and the King of Kings, the King of

Glory was born in a manger. He did not come to be served, He came to serve.

One of the reasons Jesus lived here on earth was to show us how to live. Ephesians 5:1–2 instructs us to be imitators of God and walk in love as Jesus loved us. We are called to be like Jesus, who was an example of how to be holy, without sin. And we can live holy in the twenty-first century. The power of God gives us grace and an anointing to be holy, and nothing in this world can overcome it.

After Jesus washed His disciples' feet, He instructed them and gave them—and us—a promise that hinges on a very important word, the tiny word *if*. Jesus said that *if* we *know* the things He has taught about servanthood, we will be happy if we do them. Like every promise of God, this is conditional. The condition is that we "know," which means to see, to have not only an intellectual but also a heart understanding of God's revelation to us. It means that we have taken the time to meditate on what He said, so that it is abiding in us. The result of knowing and doing His Word is that we will be happy. Jesus taught that if we follow His example and serve one another, we will be happy.

What does it mean to be happy? *Makarios*, the Greek word for "happy," means to be supremely blessed, to be fortunate, to be well off. *Webster's 1828 Dictionary* says that "happy" means being in the enjoyment of agreeable sensations from the possession of a good. The pleasurable sensations derived from the gratification of sensual appetites render a person temporarily happy, but only he who enjoys peace of mind in the favor of God can be esteemed really and permanently happy.

God does not want us to have mere temporary happiness,

which goes from mountain top to valley—I am happy, I am sad. No, He desires that we be permanently happy, no matter what is going on in our lives. It is the will of God that we be happy, emotionally happy, wearing a smile and walking with pep in our steps. He wants us to feel good, not through sin but through righteousness. God cares not only about the spirit and the body, but also about the soul—the mind, will and emotions. He does not want us to be sad, bad and disgusted. He does not want us depressed or stressed out.

The Root of Happiness

Rid me, and deliver me from the hand of strange children, whose mouth speaketh vanity, and their right hand is a right hand of falsehood: That our sons may be as plants grown up in their youth; that our daughters may be as corner stones, polished after the similitude of a palace: That our garners may be full, affording all manner of store: that our sheep may bring forth thousands and ten thousands in our streets: That our oxen may be strong to labour; that there be no breaking in, nor going out; that there be no complaining in our streets. Happy is that people, that is in such a case: yea, happy is that people, whose God is the LORD.

—Psalm 144:11–15

Psalm 34:19 says that many are the afflictions of the righteous, and David certainly understood this. He could also give testimony to the last part the verse: "but the LORD delivereth him out of them all." David offered frequent praise to God because He was faithful to deliver him from trouble. For example, in Psalm 144:1–2 he honored God as his strength and his fortress. As he neared the end of the psalm (verse 11), however, he remembered those who opposed him and began praying to God.

First, he asked God to once again deliver him from trouble. Then he prayed that God would bless him by blessing his family. In verse 12 he expressed his desire for his sons to grow up strong and vigorous. He also asked that his daughters would be beautiful and strong, as corner stones in a palace. As he continued praying, he asked that his garners—what we would call our storehouses or our bank accounts—would be full (verse 13). He prayed that his sheep would multiply abundantly. This was the same as us asking God to make our work productive.

In verse 14, David prayed that there would be "no breaking in"—divine protection from intruders. He also asked that there be no complaining, or cries of anguish, in the streets. After he had prayed for all these things, he exclaimed in verse 15, "Happy is that people, that is in such a case." Happy, he said, are those people who have been delivered by You, their family is blessed. They are blessed financially. They are walking in divine protection. That is a happy people.

And then David identified the root of this happiness, "happy is that people, whose God is the LORD." This is the key to the whole Psalm. When God is our Lord we enjoy happiness. True happiness, permanent happiness comes from God, and this is what Adam had before he sinned. After he sinned, however, there was a void in his spirit, and it has passed down to all of us. We try to fill the void with things such as money, sexual pleasure, drugs, and fame, but the only thing that will fill it up is Jesus Christ.

Anything we serve is a god to us. When we pursue something because we think it will make us happy, we have made it our god. We may achieve temporary happiness, but not true, lasting happiness. Satan deceives people with the attraction of things that offer temporary satisfaction, just like someone who sits on the back of a donkey and dangles a carrot in front of it. The donkey cannot reach the carrot, but it keeps going forward in an effort to get it. This describes people who spend their lives trying to get happiness. They may catch it every once in a while, but it does not make them happy. Then Satan pulls out another carrot, and they keep striving after happiness.

All the while, God has provided genuine happiness in Jesus. Colossians 2:10 tells us, "And ye are complete in him [Jesus], which is the head of all principality and power." The void in our lives is filled up when we receive Jesus Christ as our personal Lord and Savior. We have joy because we are complete in him. On the other hand, it is a scary thing to live in this world without Jesus. A person without Christ really has nobody to care for their problems and needs. They do not know if they will be here tomorrow, and they are afraid of many things, including death.

God's Provision That Our Joy Might Be Full

In John 15:11 Jesus said, "These things have I spoken unto you, that my joy might remain in you, and that your joy might be full." As we stated in chapter 3, this verse talks about two types of joy—*Christ's* joy and *our* joy. If we are born again, the Holy Spirit is inside us. Galatians 5:22 says that He is producing joy—Christ's joy—as well as eight other fruit. We have the joy of the Lord within us right now. Romans 5:5 teaches that the love of God is shed abroad in our hearts by the Holy Spirit, and this is also true of the joy of the Lord. It is a spiritual force that we carry within us all the time.

We do not need to reach inside to have Christ's joy when things are going good. We are already happy because we are receiving blessings from God. However, when things get tough, we must believe the promise that God wants our happiness—our joy—to remain in us. He wants our joy to be full. In John 16:24, He said, "Ask, and ye shall receive, that your joy may be full."

As we face difficult, joy-exhausting situations, we must tap into Christ's joy inside of us. It is like an emergency reserve that we can draw on when things are not going right in our lives. We do not have to be like the world and become sad and depressed in the time of trouble. We can stir up his joy on the inside, and it will bubble up and cause our joy, our happiness, to be full. The joy of the Lord will make us happy, even in hard times. That is why God has given it to us.

From the time I was growing up, I have known Christians who have modeled God's will for our joy to be full. Whenever I saw them, they were happy, joyful Christians. At first I thought they must have had a good day. After a while, I wondered, "Are they for real?" And after I had come to know them better, I could see that they were going through difficult things but their joy was still full. One of these people is a pastor I still know. To this day, he has to be the happiest person I have ever known. He always has a big smile on his face, and when he gets around you, the joy just jumps off on you.

God wants all of us to be happy, joyful Christians who tap into what God put inside us. In fact, this is one of the things that will distinguish us from those who are lost. God wants to use it to get their attention so that they will ask us about it and we can tell them about Jesus. However, when we walk around just as sad, bad, and disgusted as them, they will not be able to see a difference in our lives. People can tell what is going on in our lives by looking at our faces. They can tell if we are not allowing the joy of the Lord inside us to do its job.

When we are facing difficult situations, we need friends who will say, "That is what happened to you, but let me tell you what the Word says. You need to stir up the joy of the Lord inside you. Stop feeling bad for yourself. Remember who you serve. He is greater than your circumstance. He is the most high God."

In chapter 3, we described how David encouraged himself in the Lord at a time when he and his men had lost their families in a raid by the Amalekites. First Samuel 30 tells how they all were in great distress, and David was in danger of being stoned by his own men. Yet, in the great emotional pain he was experiencing, David stirred up the joy of the Lord inside him. He encouraged himself in the Lord and reached a place where he was feeling better. He got his joy back.

Sometimes God leads us to someone who can be a blessing to us. However, if we do not have the encouragement of other Christians available, we can, like David, encourage ourselves in the Lord by stirring up the joy He has placed within us. In Psalms 42 and 43, David spoke to his soul three times and said, "Soul, why are you disquieted? Soul, why are you cast down? Hope thou in God." And this is what he did in

1 Samuel 30. He made a decision that he would not allow himself to be depressed. He came into the presence of God and encouraged himself in God. He stirred up the joy of the Lord that was in him and chose to operate in joy. We can choose to do the same.

Joy Unspeakable and Wholehearted Praise

> Who are kept by the power of God through faith unto salvation ready to be revealed in the last time. Wherein ye greatly rejoice though now for a season, if need be, ye are in heaviness through manifold temptations...Whom having not seen, ye love; in whom, though now ye see him not, yet believing, ye rejoice with joy unspeakable and full of glory...
>
> —1 Peter 1:5–6, 8

The apostle Peter exhorted us to greatly rejoice—literally meaning to "jump for joy"—when we go through many temptations. This is the dividing line between the immature Christian and the mature Christian. The immature Christian walks around with his head down, but the mature Christian always walks around with his head up. Even if he is in trouble, he knows whom he serves! He knows that he serves the most high God, who is stronger than his circumstances. He knows that God is going to come through, so he rejoices in advance. He practices his victory dance!

We all understand what it is like to deal with many temptations. We know what it's like to have marriage needs, and also be struggling with our children at the same time. We have health problems, and we may have financial or employment needs at the same time. When this happens, we can choose to greatly rejoice and jump for joy, even when we do not feel like it. In Philippians 4:4, the apostle Paul said, "Rejoice in the Lord always: and again I say, Rejoice." As we do this, we are reminded that nothing is too hard for God. When we compare our problems to the God we serve, we can anticipate with joy the rich blessings He has provided for us.

First Peter 1:8 speaks about stirring up Christ's joy within us when it says that we "rejoice with joy unspeakable and full of glory." This is not just "Oh, hallelujah." It is like the joy David expressed when he danced with abandon before the Lord at the head of the procession that was bringing the ark of the covenant back to Israel in 1 Chronicles 15:25–29. If we had no other reason to rejoice with joy unspeakable, we could rejoice in the fact that Jesus has paid the way for us to go to heaven. We have been translated out of darkness into light.

Satan tries to trick us into staying upset and depressed when we are going through many struggles and needs. He does not want us to gain victory. However, we can stir up the joy of the Lord, so that our negative circumstances do not affect our joy and happiness. Nehemiah 8:10 reminds us that the joy of the Lord is our strength, and we can tap into this in our darkest hours. Having a pity party does not move God to act on our behalf. However, He gives us blessings and joy as we come to Him with faith that does not cry about our problems, but rejoices about God's answers.

The Bible teaches us that we are to praise God with our whole heart. When we say, "Glory be to God," we should mean "Glory be to God!" That is when the presence of God comes down and we stir up the joy of the Lord! We must guard against playing a religious game and living the Christian life in a mechanical way. When we know what to do and get used to doing it, we become tempted to just do it. However, Jesus told us to love the Lord our God with *all* our heart, *all* our soul and *all* our might. We are called to give ourselves wholeheartedly to God when we love Him, praise Him, pray to Him, and serve him. God is looking at our hearts.

When we come to God with wholehearted praise, we enter into His presence and are filled up with joy. This is what David was talking about when he said, "Thou wilt shew me the path of life: in thy presence is fulness of joy" (Psalm 16:11). This scripture does not do us any good right now if going to heaven is the only way we can come into God's presence. However, through praise, we do have access to God and the fullness of joy that His presence gives. We experience this when we worship and praise God at church. We may not be feeling well when arrive at church, and we have all kinds of problems. However, when we begin praising God, we receive the ministry of His presence and joy. We *feel* better, like a load has been lifted off.

We do not have to be in church for this to happen. Wherever we are, we can stir up the joy of the Lord. I can imagine how David responded to his seemingly impossible situation by finding a place where he could lift his hands and begin to praise and worship God. He must have reminded himself how awesome and mighty God is. He probably sang, "God you are my fortress. I know you are more than able to take care of my circumstance."

The early church taught us how to stir up joy. In Acts 3:1–8 Peter and John, by the power of God, healed a forty-year-old man who had been lame from birth. The religious authorities were very disturbed by their passionate witness for Christ and threatened them, telling them to never preach of Jesus again. Peter and John went back to their own company and then the church went to God in prayer. As Acts 4:24-28 shows, the early followers of Christ began their prayer by telling how great God is. When we come to God, we too need to enter into His presence by praising Him for His glory and His power. The joy of the Lord will start bubbling up inside us.

How to Stir Up the Joy of the Lord

We can follow three practical steps to stir up the joy of the Lord within us. First, we choose to be happy. Psalm 118:24 says, "This is the day which the LORD hath made; we will rejoice and be glad in it." We choose whether we will rejoice in God. We choose to walk around saying, "I am a happy man" or "I am a happy woman." We choose to begin our day by saying this is the day the Lord has made and I choose to be glad in it. I am going to rejoice. I am going to be happy.

Second, we come into the presence of God with praise. Because of our schedules, we tend to limit the length of our daily time with God. We say, I am going to praise God this long. I am going to pray this time and get in the Word this long. However, when we are going through tough times, we need to forget the clock. We need to say, "I am just going to stay here until I feel better, until I get my joy back up, until I am encouraged." I do not think David had a five-minute praise and worship service and was suddenly encouraged. I believe he stayed before God until he was where God wanted him to be.

Third, we pray in other tongues. 1 Corinthians 14:4 simply says, "He that speaketh in an unknown tongue edifieth himself." Jude 20 tells us to build up ourselves on our most Holy faith by praying in the Holy Ghost. When we pray in other tongues, we are charging our spiritual batteries. We are making our spirit man stronger. I can remember many times when I have felt down while I was driving in my car. The Spirit of God has reminded me, "Just pray in other tongues while you are driving." By the time I arrived at my destination and got out of the car, I felt better. I was stronger. Joy was able to reign in my life.

We return again to John 15:11 and the words He spoke to His disciples. "I am speaking this word to you," He told them, "that my joy might remain in you, and that your joy, your happiness, might be full." Jesus gave the Word to His disciples, and we read it today as the written Word of God. The apostle John repeated Christ's desire for us to be happy in 1 John 1:4: "And these things write we unto you, that your joy may be full."

The Word will fill you up with joy. When we receive the Word and start meditating on it, we begin to see what God says about our circumstances. We understand that He says we are more than conquerors, world-overcomers, and our circumstances do not determine our happiness. The Word of God fills us up with joy, because we are seeing our situations as God sees them. We stir up the joy of the Lord within us.

It is so important that we act on this provision God has made for us to be happy. We must choose to be happy and enter into His presence with praise from our hearts. Wherever we are, we can stir up the joy of the Lord in our hearts and be happy.

19:23 confirms this by saying, "The fear of the LORD tendeth to life: and he that hath it shall abide satisfied." Because we fear God, we will be satisfied not only for an occasional moment, but we will stay satisfied. We will always be filled up with the good things God gives us because we are not relying on our own ability but on Him.

God does not want us to lack any good thing. If something is good, He wants us to have it. And, of course, we also understand that God is *not* in the business of giving his people evil. Kate McVeigh describes the difference between God's role and Satan's role in the world by saying that if you add an *o* to *God*, you have the word *good*. However, if you take a *d* away from the word *devil*, you have the word *evil*. God wants us to have every good thing he has created on this planet. Genesis 1 and 2 tell how he created good things for the man and woman He made and also for all people. He does not want us to lack *any* good thing.

How do we enter the place where we lack no good thing? How do we "abide satisfied," as Proverbs 19:23 describes? Isaiah 26:3 gives the answer: "Thou wilt keep him in perfect peace, whose mind is stayed on thee: because he trusteth in thee." The phrase "perfect peace" comes from the Hebrew word *shalom*, which refers to a state in which nothing is missing and nothing is broken. God said that he will keep us in perfect peace if we trust in Him. He will not provide it for only a season, but he will keep us there. This is good news.

Psalm 115:11–14 teaches us more about God's heart to bless us:

Ye that fear the LORD, trust in the LORD: he is their help and their shield. The LORD hath been mindful of us: He will bless us. he will bless the house of Israel; he will bless the house of Aaron. He will bless them that fear the LORD both small and great. The LORD shall increase you more and more, you and your children.

—Psalm 115:11–14

We who fear the Lord are called to trust in Him as our help and our shield. We can do this with the confidence that He is mindful of us. He is thinking about how He will bless us. He promises to bless all who fear the Lord, "both small and great," the poor and the rich. God says, "If you fear the Lord, I am going to bless you. And I will bless you when you are small and then when you become great, I will keep on blessing you."

The psalmist went on to say that God will increase us more and more. Our destiny is one of increase. Our destiny is to see the promise of Proverbs 4:18, "the path of the just is as the shining light, that shineth more and more" every day. If we fear the Lord, every day is an increase day, a day where we enjoy more good things. Every day is a day where we walk in more of what God has for us.

God wants us to reach a place where we lack no good thing. He will keep increasing us until we lack no good thing, and then He will still keep increasing us. As long as we fear the Lord, that is our destiny. God wants us to prosper in every area of life, and He wants us to stay prosperous. He wants us to be in the place where we have perfect peace and receive the desires of our hearts.

Psalm 103:2 says, "Bless the LORD, O my soul, and forget not all his benefits." When the psalmist David said this, he was telling himself to bless the Lord. We need to do this as much as David because God loves us so much. He says, "I want to make sure you do not lack for any good thing, whether it be health, wealth, protection, or victory. I do not want you to lack for a wonderful family life or success on your job. I want you to have whatever is good. I want to make sure you do not lack for anything."

Romans 8:32 expresses this desire of God. It says that if God spared not his own son, but delivered him up for us all. How shall he not with him freely give us all things? We could read this verse to mean that if God gave us Jesus, which He did, how can He not give us all the other good things that come from receiving Jesus? It is His will that we receive all good things, that we lack none of them.

In Psalm 103:2 the Hebrew word for "benefits" actually means His acts or that which He has done. We must not forget the things God has already done for us or the things He is doing for us now. Verse 5 identifies one of these benefits: "Who satisfieth thy mouth with good things." The Amplified Bible says it this way, "Who satisfies your mouth [your necessity and desire at your personal age and situation]." God knows our needs and desires will change over time, and He promises to keep giving us good things until we are satisfied. God is Jehovah Too Much. He will bring us to the place where we are satisfied and then He will keep on giving until we overflow.

The Key to Receiving God's Blessings

The fear of the Lord is the key to receiving God's blessings. Proverbs 1:7 says, "The fear of the LORD is the beginning of knowledge." This does not mean that we are to be afraid of God. The word "fear" means reverence and awe. It is something we do on the inside first and then express in our outward responses, either to God or to other people. First Peter 3:1–2 speaks about this when it tells wives to submit to their husbands "with fear." The Amplified Bible renders part of verse 2: "You are to feel for him all that reverence includes." God says the same thing to husbands when He instructs them to honor their wives. The same principle applies both ways.

To say that "the fear of the Lord is the beginning of knowledge" means, according to the Hebrew, that it is the *foundation* of knowledge. The word "beginning" means the first, and it also speaks of opening or a commencement. Thus, we can say that operating in or even understanding the fear of the Lord is the beginning of operating in wisdom. It is the beginning of knowledge. To use the analogy of different levels of college courses, Wisdom 101 is entitled, "The Fear of the Lord." We need to learn the principles of the fear of the Lord before we can operate in true knowledge and wisdom in Wisdom 202 and beyond.

First Corinthians 2:14 says that "the natural man receiveth not the things of the Spirit of God." He operates according to what he can see and feel and understand with his mind. However, real knowledge and wisdom begin with the fear of the Lord, as we reverence God. This prepares us to operate in a higher level of knowledge and wisdom than the world. It was not a coincidence that Daniel, Shadrach, Meshach, and Abednego were ten times better in wisdom and understanding than the magicians and astrologers of Babylon (Dan. 1:20). The Word of God develops our minds far better than the word of man. And it starts with the fear of the Lord.

The natural man does not have the fear of the Lord. Instead, he is deceived by Satan, who has "blinded the minds of them which believe not" (2 Cor. 4:4). Natural thinking leads people to ignore the baby that is being formed in its mother's womb and then say that a woman's choice to kill the baby is a constitutional right. Homosexuality is supported by arguments that come from natural thinking, but a child can recognize that God intends for a man to be with a woman. And many in the halls of higher education deny the existence of God and nature's unmistakable declaration that He created the world and everything in it (Ps. 19:1).

And the natural man must face probing questions about the Bible. For example, how is it that men who lived in different times and places hundreds of years before Jesus came could write a hundred plus prophesies that He fulfilled in His life, death, and resurrection? Many books have been written to present the large volume of evidence that the Bible is truly God's inspired Word. And beyond that, we have the innumerable testimonies of people who have experienced God's supernatural power, exactly as He has promised in His Word.

Why does the natural man have such lack of true knowledge and wisdom? He does not start with the fear of the Lord. Are all believers walking in the fear of God? No, many of them operate according to what they can see and feel and understand with their minds. God desires that all believers fear the Lord, and He recognizes our need to receive teaching on it. Thus, in Psalm 34:11 He spoke through the psalmist David and said, "Come, ye children, hearken unto me: I will teach you the fear of the LORD."

Isaiah 11:1–5 speaks prophetically about Jesus and the way the Spirit of the Lord would rest on him in different manifestations such as the spirit of wisdom and understanding and the spirit of knowledge and of the fear of the Lord. Verse 3 tells how the Spirit of the Lord would "make him of quick understanding in the fear of the Lord." In other words, Jesus was taught and gained understanding in his earthly life. The Spirit of the Lord God taught him the fear of the Lord.

Operating in the Fear of the Lord

We already understand that the fear of the Lord is reverence for God. It is awe of Him. It starts in the heart, but we express it both in what we say and what we do. In Matthew 12:34, Jesus said, "Out of the abundance of the heart the mouth speaketh." And it is also true that our actions come out of the abundance of the heart. We know we are operating in the fear of the Lord if certain *actions* follow. If we are reverencing God and living in awe of Him, we will recognize that He is God, He is living in us, and He is always watching us. We will judge our actions with the question, Am I doing right in his sight?

Yes, God is always with us, and He is always watching us. We might say that God sees each of us as a reality television show. The Holy Ghost is the Holy Guest. Our bodies are temples of the Holy Spirit, and He is actually inside each of us. Thus, we reverence Him and do what He shows us is right in His sight. We live as if a person in a position of spiritual authority would evaluate our daily actions.

Proverbs 8:13 helps us understand what is right in God's sight. It says, "The fear of the LORD is to hate evil: pride, and arrogancy, and the evil way, and the froward mouth, do I hate." This teaches us that the fear of the Lord is more than simply not doing evil. It is to hate evil—pride, arrogance, the ungodly way in which the wicked live, and speech that has deviated from that which is good. To live in the fear of the Lord is to live like God would. It is being like him and operating in godliness. God hates evil because it hurts people and causes sickness, disease, poverty, and finally judgment in hell. If we do what is right in his sight, we will hate evil, too. We will avoid what we may call sins of commission, sins such as fornication and drunkenness.

Doing what is right in God's sight is more than *not* doing evil. It is also doing what He told us to do. Psalm 111:10 says, "The fear of the LORD is the beginning of wisdom: a good understanding have all they that do his commandments." God wants us to lack no good thing, and we have to operate in the fear of the Lord to receive the blessings He has made available to us. Just as there are sins of commission, there are also sins of omission. We must be careful that we do not operate in sins of omission by failing to obey God's commandments.

The fear of the Lord is to do his commandments. Jesus told us to go into all the world and preach the gospel to every creature (Mark 16:15). We are to win souls, but do we? Luke

18:1 teaches that men ought always to pray, but do we? We are to meditate on the Word of God day and night, but do we? Operating in the fear of the Lord is not just staying away from "big sins," as we like to call them. It is also doing the things God says we should do.

It is obvious that we should not do evil. Proverbs 16:6 tells us how not to do evil when it says, "By the fear of the LORD men depart from evil. "If we know God is always watching and we have reverence for Him, we want to do what is right in His sight. We will walk away from evil, even when we are tempted to sin. Out of reverence for God we will catch ourselves and say, "No, I can't say that. I can't do that. God is watching me and I want to be pleasing to him." Instead, we ask ourselves, "What would Jesus say? What would He do?"

If we find it difficult to walk away from evil, we need to develop a fear of the Lord. Spending time in God's Word will help us do this. Psalm 119:11 says, "Thy word have I hid in mine heart, that I might not sin against thee." The Word will bring us to a place where we operate in the fear of the Lord and the fear of the Lord will then cause us to depart from evil. As we allow this verse to change our lives, we will not sin against God, and will thereby depart from evil.

In Psalm 103:17–18, David told us that God's mercy is for those who fear him. He said:

> But the mercy of the LORD is from everlasting to everlasting upon them that fear him, and his righteousness unto children's children; To such as keep his covenant, and to those that remember his commandments to do them.

This is another promise that we can enjoy if we show our fear of God by keeping His covenant and doing His commandments. It is very important that we examine ourselves to see if we are living in obedience to God's Word. The apostle Paul corrected the Corinthian Christians for the selfishness they exhibited when they partook of the Lord's Supper. He exhorted them, "But let a man examine himself, and so let him eat of that bread, and drink of that cup" (1 Cor. 11:28). If God shows us that we have failed to do what is right in His sight, He will enable us to return to Him by His mercy and grace.

God has directed me to examine myself by sitting down with my prayer journal and writing out His assignments for me. This helps me see if I have not done His commandments. It is one way we can operate in the fear of the Lord and show reverence to Him. It reveals if we are doing what He has told us to do. Even if we do not sense the presence of God, he is with us. He is in us.

When we read God's command to depart from evil, we may not be tempted about sins such as fornication or cursing. However, there are a number of "little sins" that can keep us from entering into the place where we lack no good thing. We may have an unforgiving heart toward someone who has hurt us. Or we may come to church to receive the ministry of God's Word, but fail to really have relationships with our brothers and sisters in Christ. We may even try to stay away from them because they get on our nerves. God wants us to be close to one another, and Colossians 3:13 teaches us to forbear one another and forgive one another.

As we examine ourselves before God, He may show us other little things that hinder us from receiving His promises. Psalm

1:2–3 says that if we meditate in the law of God day and night, our leaf will not wither, and whatever we do shall prosper. Are we truly meditating in God's Word? Psalm 37:4 tells us to delight in God and he will give us the desires of our heart. Are we truly delighting in God? What kind of lifestyle do we have? Are growing in prayer? Are we giving as God directs us? Are we involved in fruitful ministry to others? Are we winning souls and discipling new believers? When we do these things, we receive the rewards that follow.

God will be faithful to speak to us about areas He wants to change in our lives. In fact, if He is not, we are not listening. Sometimes we may slip from a place of obedience, and the Lord will call us back. He does this because He gave us His laws so we can prosper. He wants us to enjoy our lives, and He wants us to be great blessings to others. Why did David say, "Taste and see. Fear the Lord and you will have no lack"? The whole point is that God does not want us to lack. The same Jesus who told the rich man what he lacked (Mark 10:17–22) lives inside us and He will tell us what we are lacking. He will teach us what we need so we can receive more fully from His hand.

When a good coach works with his players, he commends them for their strengths and also tells them what they need to learn. He acknowledges that they are already good players who are producing for the team. However, he wants to see them improve so they and the team can enjoy more success. This is how the Spirit of God works with us. He encourages us, then instructs us what lifestyle changes need to be made so that the devil will not be able to do a thing with us. God can do anything with you. I could bless you with any good thing."

A Most Important Choice

God wants us to fear Him and do what is right in his sight—with our families, on our jobs, and at church. In Leviticus 19:14 God says, "Thou shalt not curse the deaf, nor put a stumbling-block before the blind but shalt fear thy God: I am the LORD." He forbade us to curse the deaf or cause the blind to fall, things that are wrong in His sight, and then commanded us to do the opposite by choosing the fear of the Lord.

Near the end of the chapter, in verse 31, He warned against involvement in the psychic world, saying, "Regard not them that have familiar spirits, neither seek after wizards, to be defiled by them." Do not get involved with that foolishness. It is nothing but the devil trying to kill, steal, and destroy. And in verse 32 He added, "Thou shalt rise up before the hoary head, and honor the face of the old man and fear thy God." We are to fear God and reverence our elders. This is God's will.

Leviticus 25 talks about Israel's year of jubilee. As Christians, we understand that our jubilee began when Jesus died and rose again and we received him into our lives. In verse 17 God gave some financial rules and said, "Ye shall not therefore oppress one another; but thou shalt fear thy God." When God gave the law to Israel, He instructed the people on how they should relate to one another. God cares about this, and He showed it by using the last six of the ten commandments to tell the people how they should live with one another. He tells us that it is wrong in His sight if we oppress someone. Instead, He wants us to choose to fear Him.

As God gave further directions for the Year of Jubilee in verse 35 He said:

> And if thy brother be waxen poor, and fallen in decay with thee; then thou shalt relieve him: yea, though he be a stranger, or a sojourner; that he may live with thee. Take thou no usury [interest] of him or increase: but fear thy God.

God forbade the people of Israel to charge interest to other covenant people who had become poor and were dependent on their financial help. It was not right in His sight. He called His people to choose reverence and fear of the Lord instead.

And in verse 43 God told the people of Israel how to treat their brothers who had become so poor that they had sold themselves to be workers. "Thou shalt not rule over him with rigor; but shalt fear thy God," He said. The people were to treat their needy brothers as if they were hired servants, not slaves. They were not to be mean, but they were to fear God instead.

All these scriptures from Leviticus show the very clear choice we have between the fear of the Lord and disobeying His commands. God was telling His people over and over again that they should not follow the desires of their flesh. Instead, they should choose the fear of the Lord in every situation. Proverbs 1:29 describes the wicked as those who "hated knowledge and did not choose the fear of the LORD." We do not have to live as the wicked, whose judgment is pronounced in subsequent verses in Proverbs 1. Instead, we can choose the fear of the Lord, which is the key to having no lack and enjoying more and more increase.

We must choose to operate in the fear of the Lord constantly. Proverbs 23:17 says, "Let not thine heart envy sinners. But be thou in the fear of the LORD all the day long." Sinners may get to do what they want, when they want, but they are suffering the lack of God's blessings. However, the fear of the Lord will keep us from doing evil. We can choose to fear the Lord all the day, week, month, and year long until Jesus comes back.

If we choose the fear of the Lord, we will refrain from business dealings that would dishonor God. We will go out and witness with the soul winning team when the Lord tells us to do it. We will come to church an extra night during the week if God tells us to participate in a convention that is happening. We may not feel like doing something for God, but to fear the Lord is to do what is right in His sight. Regardless of what comes our way, we need to choose the fear of the Lord.

Ecclesiastes 12:13 says, "Let us hear the conclusion of the whole matter: Fear God, and keep his commandments: for this is the whole duty of man." This verse sums up the Book of Ecclesiastes and actually the whole of our existence by instructing us to simply choose to fear God and do that which is right in God's sight.

It is very similar to Jesus' response to the lawyer who asked Him to identify the greatest commandment. Jesus replied, "Love the Lord thy God with all thy heart, and with all thy soul, and with all thy mind.... Thou shalt love thy neighbour as thyself. On these two commandments hang all the law and the prophets" (Matt. 22:37–40).

The Bible is very clear in its instruction that we are to operate in the fear of the Lord. We are to do what is right in his sight by choosing what God would have us do in every situation. When we do this, we will lack no good thing.

Chapter 8

WALKING IN PERFECT PEACE

Thou wilt keep him in perfect peace, whose mind is stayed on thee: because he trusteth in thee.
—Isaiah 26:3

THE PROPHET ISAIAH gives us a wonderful promise of God's perfect peace. He tells us that God will not only give us peace, but He will also keep us in His perfect peace. The phrase "perfect peace" comes from the Hebrew words *shalom shalom*. The word *shalom* has a number of definitions—"safety, wellness, happy, friendly, welfare, health, and prosperity." Another meaning of *shalom* is simply "to have nothing missing and nothing broken." This *shalom* is God's will for us.

God wants us to abide in His peace. He wants us to walk in divine protection and health. He wants us to walk in divine wealth—to be rich financially so we can be a great blessing. He wants us to be blessed in our marriages and our families. He wants us to be happy, not only because we stir up the joy of the Lord inside us, but because of His many blessings to us. These things are important to God, and Psalm 138:8 assures us that He "will perfect that which concerneth [us]."

It is important to understand that God says He will keep us in *"perfect* peace"—the place where we are whole, with nothing missing and nothing broken. Some of us may be doing well in our families but our bodies are broken. Others of us may be doing well physically but have brokenness in our families. Yet others of us may be doing well physically and in our families, but have financial struggles. Regardless of our current situations, God can take us from where we are today and bring us to a place of *shalom*, a place where we can look at our lives and say all is well. And He can keep us there too, so that it will be our lifestyle.

When God promises to keep us in *shalom shalom*, He is speaking about what one commentary called "peace upon peace." Another commentary described it as, "All kinds of prosperity." And another added, "Happiness in this world and the one to come." The Scriptures speak of shalom in many places. For example, Psalm 35:27 says that God takes pleasure in the *shalom*—prosperity—of his servant. In Isaiah 26:3, God doubles it up.

God does not change. His will today is the same as it was in the beginning and as it will be tomorrow. In the beginning God's will for man was *shalom shalom*. There was nothing missing, nothing broken in Adam. He had peace upon peace. At the end of the Book of Revelation, there is nothing missing and nothing broken. We will have peace upon peace in heaven.

Jesus came so that we who live today can be in a place where we have nothing missing and nothing broken. We can have peace upon peace. Jesus Christ is "the same yesterday, and today, and forever" (Heb. 13:8). God wants us to have perfect peace.

Some people are afraid of placing their hope in God's promise of perfect peace. However, we are not talking about putting our hope in man, the economy, or anything this world has to offer. Instead, we are following God's will for us to hope in Him now. It does not matter how broken you were; it does not matter what damage Satan has wrought in your life. Jesus came to destroy the works of the devil, and he did his job. God is not going to just bring you into the place of perfect peace, but He is going to keep you there. People are going to look at your life and go, "How can that be?" And you will be able to say, "It is the most high God, it is the King of Kings, it is the Lord of Lords—He did this for me."

Yes, we need to believe God for perfect peace. It is His will for us. But we need to recognize the key to this: a mind that is stayed on God. Man is a three-part being. He is a spirit, he lives in a body, and he possesses a soul. The soul is made up of the mind, the will, and the emotions. Our minds must be stayed—propped up, leaning—on God. We receive no benefit from agreeing that God wants us to walk in perfect peace if we do not recognize that we need to have our minds stayed on Him. There is always a God-ward side and a man-ward side to any blessing God has for man. He wants us to have perfect peace, but our actual experience of having it is dependent on what we do with our minds.

One whose mind is stayed on God does not just think about Him in church or when he gets into trouble. Colossians 3:2

instructs us to set our affections on things above. We are to set our minds on heavenly things. What thoughts does God see on the screens of our minds? Are our thoughts stayed on him? Are our minds propped up on him? This will determine if we live in perfect peace. It is revelation that God wants to program into our spirit.

The Battle in the Mind

> For though we walk in the flesh, we do not war after the flesh: (For the weapons of our warfare are not carnal, but mighty through God to the pulling down of strong holds;) Casting down imaginations, and every high thing that exalteth itself against the knowledge of God, and bringing into captivity every thought to the obedience of Christ.
>
> —2 Corinthians 10:3–5

We are in a war. Ephesians 6:12 teaches that we are fighting against principalities, powers, the rulers of the darkness of this world, and spiritual wickedness in high places. We are battling against the forces of Satan, the spirit of antichrist in the earth. We are fighting so unbelievers can have the opportunity to receive Jesus. And because we are getting closer and closer to the end, the intensity of the battle is growing.

In 2 Corinthians 10:3–5 the apostle Paul described the spiritual warfare that is happening and plainly states that we are not warring after the flesh. He explained that our weapons are not "carnal," or natural, but mighty, spiritual weapons that are far superior to Satan's. Ephesians 6:17 says that we have the sword of the spirit, the Word of God. However, the Bible never says that Satan has a sword. As Bishop Keith A. Butler has said many times, our battle against Satan is not like a Star Wars scene where two people with lightsabers duel each other in a struggle that could go either way. No, only we who trust in Christ have lightsabers, and we know that we will win. Satan's only weapons against us are lying and deceit, which he uses to keep up from swinging at him.

We need the weapons God has provided to pull down—demolish—the strongholds or forts Satan has established in the world, our nation, and our cities. These strongholds exist in the lives of many, including believers. If we struggle with sickness, Satan has taken up a stronghold and we can demolish it by using the spiritual weapons God has given us. As 2 Corinthians 10:3–5 says, we battle the enemy by casting down—demolishing—imaginations. The word "imaginations" refers to "reasonings" or "thoughts." These thoughts of man are reflected in the ungodly philosophy Paul warned against in Colossians 2:8, and we destroy these philosophies with the Word of God. When we put the Word next to any man-made philosophy or religion, the Word will wipe it out.

As we cast down and destroy the strongholds of the enemy, we also bring every thought into captivity, into obedience or submission, to Christ. Another word for "obedience" is "compliance" or "agreement." Just as cars have to be in compliance with pollution laws, we need to bring our outlaw thoughts into compliance or agreement with the Word of God. God wants us to put our thoughts in prison and take them to rehab so that they will come out obeying the law of Christ.

And God says that He wants every thought. Genesis 6:5 helps us understand why when it tells how "God saw that the wickedness of man was great in the earth, and that every imagination of the thoughts of his heart was only evil continually." If every thought of man was evil, all he was doing was evil. In contrast, God wants every thought to be brought into captivity to Him so that evil does not take root in our hearts. Whatever is in our hearts determines what we will do. This is why it is so important for God's Word to abide in our hearts, that we might operate in obedience to God.

The Renewing of Our Minds

As we engage in spiritual warfare, we must remember the master key to perfect peace: keeping our minds stayed on God. Romans 12:2 teaches us how to do this when it says, "And be not conformed to this world: but be ye transformed by the renewing of your mind." God is telling us that we should not conform our lives to the lifestyle of the world. We should not copy the attitudes and actions of people who dishonor God with their lives. Instead of us trying to be like them, they need to become like us as we become like Christ. The fear of the Lord is to hate evil (Proverbs 8:13). If we hate evil, we get as far away from it as we can.

God does not want us to be conformed to the world. Rather, He desires that we be transformed by the renewing of our minds. *Metamorphoo*, the Greek word for "transformed," means changed. God is saying, "Don't live like the world; change." He wants us to change the way we live so that we are like Jesus. Ephesians 4:22-24 talks about this when it says to put off the old man, the old way of living, and put on the new man. We know God wants us to do this, but many of us become stuck in the transition because we do not understand the power of the mind.

When we are saved, God gives each of us a brand new spirit. However, our minds have to be renewed, retrained, reprogrammed not only in what we know, but also in how we think. We need to consider what will result from the input that goes into our minds. We do not just renew our minds because we come to church and hear the Word; we actually have to reprogram our minds so that we are thinking like Jesus wants us to think, not like the world.

It is no coincidence that Ephesians 4:22 has the phrase "be renewed in the spirit of your mind" between the actions of putting off the old man and putting on the new man. A battle is raging in the life of every believer. As Jesus told His disciples in Matthew 26:41, the spirit is willing, but the flesh is weak. Our spirit wants to do what is right, but our flesh wants to do what is wrong. Our mind determines what we actually do. If our spirit controls our thinking, we will do what our spirit says. But if our flesh controls our thinking, we will do what our flesh says.

Romans 8:5–6 talks about this:

> For they that are after the flesh do mind the things of the flesh; but they that are after the Spirit the things of the Spirit. For to be carnally minded is death; but to be spiritually minded is life and peace.

A carnal Christian is carnally- or fleshly-minded. A carnal Christian thinks according to the flesh, and the flesh thinks the way the world thinks. However, when we are born again, we begin a renewal process. This is why we come to church, open our Bibles, and listen to the Word of God. We are retraining ourselves to think spiritually, not carnally. We are learning to remove the flesh from the throne of our minds and put the new spirit God has given us there instead. As we do this, we become spiritually-minded—mature—and have life and peace.

We must ask ourselves who controls our thoughts. Is it God or Satan? Is it our flesh or our spirit? If we monitor our thoughts and then look at our lives we will see a surprising correlation between what we think and what we do. And, of course, what we do has an impact on how we live. The stakes are high. The more we give God our thoughts, the more we will walk in perfect peace. If we want 100 percent peace— that is what God wants is to have—we have to give Him 100 percent of our lives. We have to let Him be Lord over all our thoughts. The more we think and live the Word, the more benefits we receive.

Guarding Against Ungodly Thoughts

When we open ourselves to the Word of God, it goes straight into our hearts. On the other hand, the mind is Satan's doorway into our hearts. God warns us against giving place to the devil (Eph. 4:27), and He tells us to deny him access by aligning every thought in compliance with His Word. If a person ignores or rejects this direction from God and meditates on evil thoughts, evil will take root in his heart and bear the fruit of unrighteousness. As Jesus said in Matthew 15:19–20, "For out of the heart proceed evil thoughts, murders, adulteries, fornications, thefts, false witness, blasphemies: These are the things which defile a man."

This is why we must guard against ungodly things that enter

our minds through our eyes and our ears. Whatever we see or hear over and over becomes rooted in our minds and drops into our hearts. And then we begin expressing it in our words and deeds. Satan cannot place evil directly into our hearts, but he attacks us with thoughts such as, "Oh, she looks good....And nobody knows where you are right now." Or he will say, "You don't have to give God a tithe this time around. He knows what you're going through."

The whole area of hurts is fertile soil for Satan to sow evil in our lives. He reminds us over and over about wrongs we have suffered and the people who offended us. As the situation grows larger and larger in our minds, we tell ourselves, "I don't know why they did that to me. That's the second time they were so unkind." Sometimes we tell others about the offense too and infect them with the bitter poison that has taken root in our lives. The result is that we lose the peace God has provided for us and fall prey to other forms of evil.

Ephesians 6:10 and 16 instructs us to put on the whole armor of God so we can stand against the wiles of the devil and quench his fiery darts. We tend to think, and rightly so, that these fiery darts are sickness, disease, and persecution. However, Satan attacks the ministry of the Word in other ways too, as Mark 4:15–19 teaches:

> And these are they by the way side, where the word is sown; but when they have heard, Satan cometh immediately, and taketh away the word that was sown in their hearts. And these are they likewise which are sown on stony ground; who, when they have heard the word, immediately receive it with gladness; And have no root in themselves, and so endure but for a time: afterward,

when affliction or persecution ariseth for the word's sake, immediately they are offended. And these are they which are sown among thorns; such as hear the word, And the cares of this world, and the deceitfulness of riches, and the lusts of other things entering in, choke the word, and it becometh unfruitful.

In Mark 4:1–20 Jesus told the story of the sower who sowed the Word into the hearts of four groups of people. Three of these groups did not bear fruit because of Satan's attacks against them. As we begin reading this story, we learn that the enemy came and immediately stole the word that had been sown into the people by the wayside. This group represents people who do not open up their hearts to receive the Word. Second Corinthians 4:4 speaks about this group and says, "The god of this world hath blinded the minds of them which believe not." Because they do not open up their hearts to the Word, Satan does not have to do anything special. He just comes and takes it.

Satan sent affliction and trouble against the second group. Affliction, which may be sickness, disease, financial trouble, persecution, and even people, offends those who are represented by this group, and they fall away. This does not have to happen, however, because we will have victory over this attack if we walk in faith through times of trouble.

However, Satan is slippery. If he cannot stop the ministry of God's Word by his first two methods, he will attack in a subtle way, as he did against the third group. He will sow three kinds of thorns: the cares of the world—anxieties and distractions; the deceitful perception that riches—money and wealth—are the answer to all our problems; and the "lusts of other things"—

inordinate strong desires for things instead of God. When these things enter the hearts of people represented by this group, they choke the Word and it does not produce fruit.

The enemy's evil works against the third group illustrate why God is so insistent that every thought be in obedience to Christ. Satan has access to our minds, and he will attack us with thoughts that will rob us of perfect peace. The issue is not that these thoughts come through our minds, but that we hang on to them and keep thinking about them. Genesis 3:1-6 shows the danger of this in the story of the temptation of Adam and Eve:

> Now the serpent was more subtil than any beast of the field which the LORD God had made. And he said unto the woman, Yea, hath God said, Ye shall not eat of every tree of the garden? And the woman said unto the serpent, We may eat of the fruit of the trees of the garden: But of the fruit of the tree which is in the midst of the garden, God hath said, Ye shall not eat of it, neither shall ye touch it, lest ye die. And the serpent said unto the woman, Ye shall not surely die: For God doth know that in the day ye eat thereof, then your eyes shall be opened, and ye shall be as gods, knowing good and evil. And when the woman saw that the tree was good for food, and that it was pleasant to the eyes, and a tree to be desired to make one wise, she took of the fruit thereof, and did eat, and gave also unto her husband with her; and he did eat.

When Satan tempted Adam and Eve, he appeared to them as a serpent. In his first words to Eve, he questioned God's Word, just as he does today. Then he went a step further and called God a liar. "If you eat of it," Satan said, "you will not die. What

God said is not really true." Satan lies to us about God and the rich blessings He has for us. He tells us, "You are not going to make it. You are going to be sick and die." He is trying to see what lies we will accept, and if he can see that we will listen to some, he will come back and go a step farther. Like the saying goes, if you give him an inch he will take a country mile; let him in the backseat and soon he will be driving.

Eve received Satan's lie. She did not say, "No, no, God said in the day I eat thereof I shall surely die. Adam!" She did not do that. She said, "Oh"—then she turned and looked at the forbidden fruit. She already knew the tree was good for food. She looked at it again, "Ooh, that looks good. It's pretty." And then she took the fruit and ate it and gave some to Adam. This is how Satan began his temptation of people, and it is the way he still operates. He does not have any new tricks.

The temptation of Adam and Eve shows that we need to have a "spiritual customs agent" at the door of our mind. We need to check our thoughts to see if they are of God or of Satan. If they are of God we will let them in; if they are not of God we will kick them out. This is what Jesus did. When Satan introduced the temptation that He turn stones into bread, Jesus did not consider it even for a moment. He said, "No, it is written..." and spoke the Word of God. In the third temptation recorded in Matthew 4:1–11, Jesus said "Get behind me, Satan." Instead of receiving the thought, he dealt with the source.

Each time Satan tempted Jesus, our Lord responded with the Word. This is what we have to do when thoughts that are not of God come our way. As we examine our thoughts and recognize that they are not of God, we must speak God's Word against the enemy. We fight thoughts with the Word of God. This is how we cast down imaginations and demolish them.

Breaking the Pattern of Wrong Thinking

The human mind is made in such a way that we cannot think one thing and say another. Therefore, when Satan attacks our thoughts, he is persistent. If we have a pattern of wrong thinking, we will have to be just as persistent in the battle to renew and retrain our minds. When Satan introduces an ungodly thought, we have to audibly rebuke it and speak the Word of God about it. If Satan tells us that we are not going to make it financially, we must say, "No, I rebuke that thought. My God shall supply all my needs." If he suggests that we commit immorality with someone, we must respond, "No, I rebuke that thought. The Word of God told me to flee fornication."

When we speak the Word of God against Satan's thoughts, he does not have a sword to battle against it. He may keep coming back for awhile, as he did when he tempted Jesus. However, as we follow Jesus' pattern and keep saying, "It is written, The time will come when he will depart for a season" (Luke 4:13). However, we cannot just receive ungodly thoughts and think about them because it will allow Satan to rob our happiness. All may be well, but thinking about the one thing we wish were different will lead to covetousness. If we listen to the enemy's thoughts over and over, we will find ourselves in a place of great loss and wonder how we got there.

Scripture shows the pattern by which Satan brings destruction to the lives of those who listen to his evil thoughts. Acts

4:34–37 tells about a season in the church at Jerusalem when the Holy Spirit moved some of the believers to sell their lands and houses and give the proceeds to the ministry of the church. Acts 5:1–11 tells how Ananias and Sapphira sold some property, but they also decided, "Let's lie; let's say that we sold the land for this much and keep the rest of the money." They wanted to look spiritual like everyone else who was selling their lands or houses and giving generously to the church.

When Ananias came to give the money to the apostles, God revealed to Peter that Ananias had lied about the price he received for his land. Peter said, "Ananias, why hath Satan filled thine heart to lie to the Holy Ghost?" (Acts 5:3). He recognized that Satan was behind the lie. And where did it start? It began with a thought that dropped in the hearts of Ananias and Sapphira, and it cost them their lives.

We see this pattern again in the life of Judas Iscariot. Matthew 26:6–16 tells how a woman poured an alabaster box of very costly ointment on Jesus' head as He was sitting in the house of Simon the Leper. The disciples—especially Judas—were very upset about this, and said that it might have been sold to give money to the poor. Jesus, however, told them to leave her alone, for she had done a good work. The next thing we read is that Judas went to the religious leaders to make an agreement in which he would turn Jesus over to them for money.

Judas was the treasurer, and he had already been stealing money out of the treasury. Satan had already established that sin as a stronghold in his life, and he took him to the final step. As John 13:2 says, Satan put in the heart of Judas to betray Jesus. How did Satan get into his heart like that? Scripture does not say that Satan has access to our hearts, but it does show

how he can bring ungodly thoughts our way. This is what led Judas to the place of betraying Jesus. He was with Jesus every day for three and a half years. He saw miracle after miracle and heard teaching after teaching. We know Jesus taught against covetousness (Mark 7:22), but Judas failed to follow Christ's words because he allowed Satan to reign in his thoughts.

We must examine our minds to see what thoughts we have been thinking? Have we been thinking the Word or thinking our trouble? Whatever we are thinking will be rooted in our hearts. Whatever is rooted in our hearts will become our attitudes and actions. If we keep doubt in your minds, it will eventually move into our hearts and create fear. And where fear begins faith ends.

So what do we do? First Peter 5:8–9 says, "Be sober, be vigilant; because your adversary the devil, as a roaring lion, walketh about, seeking whom he may devour: Whom resist stedfast in the faith." God, speaking through the apostle Peter, is warning us: "Don't be drunk, don't have your senses dulled. Instead, be spiritually alert; be on guard because Satan, your adversary, wants to kill you, steal from you, and destroy you." He tells us that the devil walks about as a roaring lion, looking for Christians he may devour. Just like the Lord searches throughout the Earth for those He can strengthen, Satan walks back and forth throughout the Earth to find vulnerable Christians he can afflict and destroy (Job 1:6–12).

Satan is unable to devour Christians who are alert and vigilant. However, he is able to do great harm to those who are not alert, those who are caught up in the things of this world a little too much. A lion may take down an animal bigger than itself, an elephant perhaps, if that animal is vulnerable. But if the elephant is looking at him, he may not go after it. That is a picture of Satan. He finds the Christian who is not guarding his thought life and tells him, "God did not really mean that." He begins the process of destruction in the vulnerable ones. However, he knows that believers who are sober and vigilant can, through God's power, crush him under their feet (Rom. 16:20).

God directs us to oppose Satan and stand against him. To walk in perfect peace, we have to stay alert spiritually and resist ungodly thoughts. We cannot receive the thought, but we must choose to bring every thought unto the captivity of Christ. If a thought does not line up with Christ, we are to capture it and bring it in line with Christ and His Word. We resist thoughts from the enemy by audibly rebuking them. We speak the Word of God and resist every single attack from Satan. As Ephesians 4:27 instructs us, we do not give place to the devil.

How Perfect Peace Prevails

Worry is one area where Satan attacks our thoughts. Philippians 4:6 tells us how to respond to this and exhorts us, "Be careful for nothing." We should not even have one thought of worry. If a thought of worry comes our way, we have to recognize that it is from the enemy and make it captive to Christ. The world operates with the belief that it is responsible to worry, and our flesh wants to worry because it is uncertain about things. But God says, He does not want you to worry about anything.

Even though we experience some strong influences on our thought life, we control it. This is why God commanded us, "Do not worry about anything." It is why Jesus said in Matthew 6:25 and 33, "Do not think about what you will eat or drink, do not think about what you will put on or any of those things. Instead, think about the kingdom of God and His righteousness and I will add all these things to you. You will have perfect peace" (author's paraphrase). Yes, we control what we think. We just have to retrain our minds so that our natural response will change from worry to the action of rebuking ungodly thoughts and believing in God. He is faithful, true, awesome, and able, and He will do what He said He will do.

Philippians 4:8 gives us positive direction on how to respond to thoughts of worry. Instead of thinking bad thoughts, we are to think on whatever is true, honest (honorable), just, pure (clean), lovely (acceptable), and of good report (reputable). When we look at our circumstances we see facts, but the Word is the truth. It is everything this verse teaches us to keep central in our thoughts. As we think on God's Word, our thoughts will be of good report. If people could look at them, they would commend them as good. God, of course, sees and knows all our thoughts. Does He see thoughts that influence us to receive His perfect peace?

The conclusion of Philippians 4:8 says, "whatsoever things are of good report; if there be any virtue [excellence] and if there be any praise [laudation], think on these things." God tells us how to live and He tells us how to think. He says, "think on," meditate on, take inventory of God and His Word. When thoughts come to our minds, we have to ask if they are true, honorable, pure, and of good report. If they are, we must think on them. If they are not, we must reject them.

Because the Word of God fits Philippians 4:8 in its entirety, we are to meditate on it day and night. The psalmist said that God's Word was his meditation all the day (Psalm 119:97).

I have found that when I am not listening to the Word as much as I should—at church, on a tape or CD, by reading a book—my thought life is not in the Word. But if I am sitting under the Word of God I will think about what the Word has to say. I will start thinking about the Word versus my problems. The Word of God should be our main mental diet.

God makes the promise of perfect peace to all whose minds are stayed on Him. When we set our thoughts and affections on His Word, on His kingdom, on things above, we are able to obey Jesus' instruction that we should not think about what we are going to eat or drink or what we are going to wear (Matt. 6:25). Instead, He tells us in verse 33 to seek kingdom things first. We are to think about what God's Word says and about His assignment for us in our families. We are to consider what we can do to help the kingdom of God expand by winning the lost and helping other believers. We are to seek after things that cause God's will to be accomplished throughout this earth. Our minds are stayed on him and we are qualified for perfect peace.

The key to walking in perfect peace is that we let God be Lord of our every thought. The psalmist David understood this and he expressed it eloquently in Psalm 19:14. Let us join him in praying, "Let the words of my mouth, and the meditation of my heart, be acceptable in thy sight, O LORD, my strength, and my redeemer."

Chapter 9

WALKING IN HUMILITY

Put on therefore, as the elect of God, holy and beloved, bowels of mercies, kindness, humbleness of mind, meekness, longsuffering.
—Colossians 3:12

WE AS BELIEVERS face challenges on two levels. When we are first born again we often face level-one challenges. As we grow in God, we move on to level-two challenges. And as we mature in Christ through these challenges, we prosper like God wants us to prosper.

When the apostle Paul wrote to the Colossians, he listed some level-one challenges: "fornication, uncleanness, inordinate affection, evil concupiscence, and covetousness, which is idolatry" (Col. 3:5). There was a time when we walked in these sins, but we should not be living in them now. We need to be in the place where our flesh is not ruling us, particularly in sins such as fornication, adultery, homosexuality, murder, and stealing.

A few verses later, Paul identified some level-two challenges, including "anger, wrath, malice [evil intent], blasphemy, filthy communication out of your mouth" (Col. 3:8). If we tear someone down with our words, we are guilty of filthy communication. And in the following verse, Paul reminded us, "Lie not one to another" (Col. 3:9)

We should not be involved in level-one sins or level-two sins, but we must also receive and practice God's instruction to put on the opposite action of the level two sins. Colossians 3:12 lists some of these opposites as mercy, kindness, humility of mind, meekness, and longsuffering. Mercy is the opposite of malice, and kindness is the opposite of filthy communication. The third action identified is humility of mind, which is the opposite of pride.

We as believers may have died to the "big sins." However, God sees any and all sin as sin. We may not be involved with level-one sins, but we may be walking in pride. Maybe we have laid hands on someone and they were healed. Or maybe we have been serving in a church ministry for many years. We are tempted to puff ourselves up and look down on unbelievers and new believers. God is not pleased with this, and He calls us to overcome the temptation of pride by putting on humility of mind.

Walking in humility is the key to walking in total prosperity and abiding satisfied. It is very important because Satan is subtle. Sometimes we become prideful when we talk about pride. We may say, "Well, I am not proud." It is imperative that we examine ourselves to see if we are really as humble as we think we are.

James, the pastor of the Jerusalem church, provided a standard for us to measure our humility. Writing in the New Testament book that bears his name, he addressed the fact that believers were fighting one another and said, "From whence come wars and fightings among you? come they not hence, even of your lusts that war in your members?" (James 4:1). Paul also spoke against this in his first letter to the Corinthians. He noted that there were divisions in the church and said, in effect, "You are still carnal" (1 Cor. 3:3, author's paraphrase).

Why were these early Christians fighting each other? They were fighting for things they desired, and honor was part of what they wanted. This strong desire for honor brought death to Ananias and Sapphira. As we explained in chapter 8, they sold some of their land and kept part of the proceeds for themselves. However, when they came to give their gift, they lied and said they were giving the full sale price. They wanted to look spiritual and receive honor, but they suffered God's judgment instead.

Each of us must ask ourselves searching questions about our words and actions: Why did I say that? Why do I do what I do? Why am I in this specific ministry? Did God call me to be serve Him in ministry where I am seen, or did He call me to serve Him where I cannot be seen? When people do not see our service for Christ, we are not likely to receive honor and praise. However, it is important that we serve God in the area to which He has called us, even if others do not see our ministry.

Humility Defined

The Greek word for *humility* means "humiliation of mind," i.e., modesty. It is also translated as "humbleness of mind." The Greek word for "humble" means depressed, not emotionally but in the sense of being pushed down (i.e., figuratively lowered in circumstances or disposition). It is also translated as "base, cast down, of low degree or state, lowly." *Vine's Expository Dictionary* defines *humility* as lowliness of mind.[1]

As I studied these definitions, two words caught my attention. The words "meek" and "lowly" were translated differently, but many times they were the same Greek word. We see this in Matthew 11:28–29, where Jesus said:

> Come unto me, all ye that labour and are heavy laden, and I will give you rest. Take my yoke upon you, and learn of me; for I am meek [exhibiting humility and patience, to be submissive] and lowly [the same Greek word for humble] in heart.

Jesus was simply saying, "I am humble." He was confident and knew who He was, but He was humble. In John 11:25 Jesus told Martha, "I am the resurrection, and the life." In John 14:6 he said, "I am the way, the truth, and the life: no man cometh unto the Father, but by me."

Webster's Dictionary defines *humility* as the quality or condition of being humble. It says that the word means "characterized by modesty or meekness in behavior, attitude or spirit" and goes on to talk about being submissive and not pretentious. Humility is of the mind and heart. As we just noticed, Webster's Dictionary says that it is "characterized by modesty or meekness in attitude or spirit." When the Bible talks about humility, it is speaking about our attitude and our spirit. God says we need to be lowly in mind and heart, humble of mind and heart.

Being humble does not means considering ourselves as less than nothing. It does not mean degrading ourselves and saying that we are just like the dirt on the ground. No, we can be confident in who we are: world overcomers, more than conquerors, called by God to have wisdom and understanding ten times greater than the unbeliever (Dan. 1:20), and able to do all things through Christ who strengthens us. Humility is essential for all these things to be true because we recognize that everything we are is because of God. Even Jesus said He could do nothing of Himself (John 5:19).

However, in Romans 12:3 the apostle Paul said that we should not think of ourselves more highly than we ought. Even though we are born again, washed in the blood, and Spirit-filled, that does not mean we are any better than the sinner. The same blood that washed away our sins and paid for our salvation paid for the worst sinner on earth. No higher price can be paid for something than the blood of Jesus, and He paid it for all of us, whether we are born again or lost in sin. We are all extremely valuable to God and have equal value in the sight of God.

Grace for the Humble

As we said earlier in this chapter, walking in humility is the key to walking in total prosperity. James 4:6 teaches this when it says, "But [God] giveth more grace. Wherefore he saith,

God resisteth the proud, but giveth grace unto the humble." One of the definitions for *grace* is "the anointing of God, the power of God." If we want to receive God's power and anointing that will enable us to walk in total prosperity, we must learn to walk in humility. If we want to live with nothing missing and nothing broken, enriched in every area of life, we must put on humility.

God resists the proud. As the meaning of the word "resisteth" shows, He opposes the proud. It is very evident that God does not want us to be proud. And, to our great benefit, it is also very clear that He is still giving grace. Second Corinthians 9:8 says, "And God is able to make all grace abound toward you; that ye, always having all sufficiency in all things may abound to every good work." This promise holds great value for us. Because God gives us grace, we always have "all sufficiency in all things." The word *sufficiency* means self-satisfaction in all things. Grace will also provide healing, victory, a mate, and a promotion for those who are believing for these things. God uses grace to grant us whatever we desire from Him.

The ministry of God's grace also works to make us "enriched in every thing" (2 Cor. 9:11). God wants us to be made rich in every area of life. He loves giving His people grace, and He desires to give us His power so we can prosper. In chapter 3 we saw that "The eyes of the Lord run to and fro throughout the whole earth to shew himself strong in the behalf of them whose heart is perfect towards him" (2 Chron. 16:9). He is looking for people who will receive His grace.

In Hebrews 4:16 God invites us to "come boldly unto the throne of grace, that we may obtain mercy, and find grace to help in time of need." James 1:5 teaches that God gives to all men liberally, and He does not hold back. He says, "Come and ask of me if you need grace" (author's paraphrase). God loves to give his people grace. The grace of God is the answer to any need we may have. It is the power of God, and He wants to give it to us.

God wants all of us to enjoy the benefits of His grace. However, we must put ourselves in a position to receive it. When James 4:6 says that God resists the proud, it means that He does not give grace to the proud. If He is opposing them, He surely is not giving to them. Being proud disqualifies us from getting grace, the power of God. But being humble puts us in a perfect position for God to pour His grace out on our lives. It enables us to receive the prosperity that comes with His grace. Yes, God wants us to be humble. He wants us to be a part of an elite group of people called "the humble."

James 4:10 says, "Humble yourselves in the sight of the Lord, and he shall lift you up." If we humble ourselves, God will take us from where we are and lift us up. This is what He did with a young man who was watching his father's sheep. In one day He took David from being a shepherd to defeat the Philistine giant Goliath and become the captain of an army. God also took a man by the name of Joseph from the jailhouse to the penthouse in one day and made him the number two ruler in the nation of Egypt. And another time, in a famine so great that people were eating their children, God acted in one day and brought them to a time of feasting (2 Kings 6:24–7:20).

God is an expert in taking us from where we are right now and lifting us up to a place where we are honored and prosperous. This is what he wants to do for us, but we must humble ourselves to get there. God wants us to be a part of the humble because they walk in total prosperity. It is also the humble who produce for God, raise the dead, cast out demons, heal the sick, and raise mighty seed. Grace not only comes on the side of prosperity, but also on the side of ministry. Grace gives us the baptism of the Holy Spirit and the power to be a witness. If we want to have the anointing to minister to people, we have to be humble.

Practical Teaching From the Apostle Peter

If we want grace to be a good husband or wife and to raise our children, we have to become humble, lowly in heart and mind, and submissive. We do not like the word *submissive*, but that is what humble people are. Instead of striving for honor with a proud heart, we must become humble. The apostle Peter taught about this:

> Likewise, ye younger, submit yourselves unto the elder. Yea, all of you be subject one to another, and be clothed with humility: for God resisteth the proud, and giveth grace to the humble. Humble yourselves therefore under the mighty hand of God, that he may exalt you in due time: Casting all your care upon him; for he careth for you. Be sober, be vigilant; because your adversary the devil, as a roaring lion, walketh about, seeking whom he may devour: Whom resist stedfast in the faith.
>
> —1 Peter 5:5–9

These verses, which are similar to James 4:6, 7, and 10, give added emphasis to the truth that walking in humility is the key to walking in prosperity. Verse 5 clearly shows that all of us—both mature believers and baby believers—are to submit to one another. We are all exhorted to be clothed with humility and, as Colossians 3:12 says, put on humbleness of mind. It is very important that we always be clothed with humility. If we find that we cannot submit to someone God has placed in a position of authority, we have pride in our lives. We have areas where we are high-minded.

This can happen in a church when the pastor declares God's plan for ministry and some of the people resist it. If the church leadership asks someone to sit and receive for a time before he begins serving in the church, he may react with the proud attitude that he should be able to serve God whenever he wants. Or pride may be revealed when people refuse to obey practical directions to make a right turn from a right-only turn lane when they leave the parking lot.

When we have a measure of success, we may become proud. This is one factor that will keep us from reaching the next level of prosperity or the next level in our career. In these situations, we may feel frustrated because we have been trying to break through what we believe is a glass ceiling. However, it may be that God is not going to move us to the next level until we are ready. We see this in 1 Timothy 3:6, which warns against placing a novice in the office of bishop "lest being lifted up with pride he fall." An immature believer is not ready to serve in the position of pastor because he may become proud if he receives the praise of men.

As we consider the relationship of pride to ministry, it is important to recognize that God knows where we are in our development. He is not going to elevate us in anointing or in what the anointing will produce until we learn the lessons we need to be successful in that position. Luke 16:10 Jesus said, "He that is faithful in that which is least is faithful also in much." We have to prove to God that we can handle our current success with humility before He gives us greater success. Proverbs 1:32 says that "the prosperity of fools shall destroy them," and God does not want us to be destroyed.

When we humble ourselves before God, He will exalt us in the time He chooses. We have to make ourselves low so we can be raised higher. As we humble ourselves and are lowly in heart, we become smaller targets for the devil and are able to resist him. However, when we walk in pride, we make ourselves large targets for the enemy. We can learn a lesson from the police officer who makes himself as small as possible if he suspects that someone might shoot at him in a gun battle. He crouches and peeks around the corner so that the one resisting his authority will have the least target to hit.

As we learn to be humble in our relationship with God, we enjoy the provision of His care for us. We cast all our cares upon Him. But if we are anxious and worried about our problems and choose to carry them instead of giving them over to God, we walk in pride. God says that we should not worry about anything. Cast your care on Him. Come to Him and He will take care of it. He calls us to walk in humility, not pride.

To be proud is to be high-minded toward God. In Isaiah 55:8–9 God shows the error of this: "For my thoughts are not your thoughts, neither are your ways my ways...For as the heavens are higher than the earth, so are my ways higher than your ways, and my thoughts than your thoughts." We may have a high level of intelligence, many academic degrees, and a wealth of life experiences, but God's knowledge and understanding is much greater than ours. Therefore, to resist what God says is to operate in pride. When we do it, we are really telling God, "I know better than You."

God's will is that we be humble and submit to Him and everything He says. He may tell us to get up earlier and pray a little extra one morning. Do we obey Him in humility? In Hebrews 10:25 He warns that we should not forsake the assembling of ourselves together. Do we come together with others in humility at His command? God may speak to us about a specific situation and instruct us to do His will in it. Do we, out of a humble heart, say yes?

We all have some measure of pride, and we show this by arguing with Him when He tells us to do something we do not want to do. It is very important that we remember who God is. He sees the end from the beginning and has our best interests at heart. If we submit to Him in humility, we will find prosperity and production for Him. Many times we resist God because of what we see with our eyes. However, if we are humble in spirit, we will submit to God like Peter did when Jesus called to him in the raging storm and invited him to come and walk to Him on the water. In Matthew 14:29 Peter, by faith, stepped out toward Jesus. We will cast all our cares on him and step out in obedience to Him.

Jesus was tempted at every point like we are, and He understands the temptation of pride (Heb. 4:15). However, in each temptation, He submitted Himself to the Father's will. The humble submit to God and his Word. They submit to the direction of the Holy Spirit. They submit to people God has put in authority over them and "one to another" (Eph. 5:21). Being clothed with humility means being submissive.

The Blessings of Humility

> At the same time came the disciples unto Jesus, saying, Who is the greatest in the kingdom of heaven? And Jesus called a little child unto him, and set him in the midst of them, And said, Verily I say unto you, Except ye be converted, and become as little children, Ye shall not enter into the kingdom of heaven. Whosoever therefore shall humble himself as this little child, the same is greatest in the kingdom of heaven.
>
> —Matthew 18:1–4

When Jesus' disciples asked Him who was greatest in the kingdom of heaven, He called a little child to come and be with them. Then, after prefacing His answer with "verily," or truly, to show that He was about to say something very important, He taught that we must be converted and become like little children to enter the kingdom of heaven. With the child in their midst, He showed the disciples what it means to be converted—changed—and come into the kingdom of heaven. He said that they must humble themselves and become like that child.

And then He answered the question His disciples had asked. He said that those who will be greatest in the kingdom of heaven must humble themselves as little children. The humility of little children is shown in their relationships to others. They do not care what people think about them., and they are not trying to gain honor. We must learn to practice this in our church relationships. We often judge each other according to where we serve Him or what we do. However, God does not look at this, but at our hearts to see if we are humble.

Humility results in many blessings. First, it gives us entrance into the kingdom of heaven. We must humble ourselves to be saved. We must come to God and say, "I now humble myself and you are my Lord. I will do what you tell me to do." The man in Mark 10:17-27 was not willing to do this. When Jesus told him to sell his possessions and give the proceeds to the poor, he went away sad.

After this conversation, Jesus told His followers that it is very difficult for those who trust in riches to come into the kingdom of God. He compared it to a camel going through the eye of a needle, a small entrance into a city. A camel had to get down almost on his knees to go though a needle. In the same way, a rich man has to humble himself to enter into the kingdom of God. The possession of money can lead easily to pride and hinder humility before God.

Proverbs 22:4 identifies three more blessings of humility: "By humility and the fear of the Lord are riches and honour and life." Humility gives us riches—not just money, but grace. It also leads to honor, not the kind that comes from boasting about ourselves but that which follows humble service to God and the people He places in our lives. And finally, humility produces life, which includes health.

And Job 22:29 teaches about another blessing of humility: "When men are cast down, then thou shalt say, There is lifting up; and he shall save [deliver, bring out] the humble person." We all face battles in life, and we may feel depressed because things are tough. However, if we are humble, we have the promise that his humility will bring us to a place of deliverance from our difficulties. We, through humility, will be set free.

Satan is always attacking, always trying to get us in a bind. The good news is that we can overcome the difficulties that come against us when we are humble. Psalm 34:19 says, "Many are the afflictions of the righteous: but the LORD delivereth him out of them all." Proverbs 12:13 promises that "the just shall come out of trouble." Even when we face persecution and famine and lack and danger and tribulation, whatever Satan sends our way, in all these things we are more than conquerors through him that loved us (Rom. 8:35, 37).

First Corinthians 10:13 says that the temptations we suffer are common to man. In other words, many people have experienced what we are going through. We all have trouble of one kind or another, even though Satan tries to deceive us into believing that we are all alone in our struggles. For this reason, we need to be sensitive to our brothers and sisters who are facing difficulties. As we join with them and come to God in humility together, they can receive deliverance and freedom from His hand.

We must not forget yet another blessing of humility described in 2 Chronicles 7:14: "If my people, which are called by my name, shall humble themselves, and pray, and seek my face, and turn from their wicked ways; then will I hear from heaven, and will forgive their sin, and will heal their land." This verse instructs us to humble ourselves in prayer to God. As we seek Him and turn from our wicked ways, He will hear our prayers and heal our land. He will bring us back to a place of prosperity. This is God's promise for those who are the humble, and we need its fulfillment more than anything else today.

It is so important that we choose to be humble. To do this, we must monitor our thoughts and our actions to be sure that we are lowly in mind and heart. We must be humble in all our relationships—with God and with the people He has placed in our lives. As we do, we will find that God gives grace unto the humble. And as we allow more grace to move in our lives, we will have greater victory.

Chapter 10

ENJOYING A RICH LIFE

How happy are those who fear the Lord—all who follow his ways! You will enjoy the fruit of your labor. How happy you will be! How rich your life!
—Psalm 128:1–2, NLT

But this I say, He which soweth sparingly shall reap also sparingly; and he which soweth bountifully shall reap also bountifully. Every man according as he purposeth in his heart, so let him give; not grudgingly, or of necessity: for God loveth a cheerful giver. And God is able to make all grace abound toward you; that ye, always having all sufficiency in all things, may abound to every good work.
—2 Corinthians 9:6–8

GOD WANTS US to enjoy a rich and abundant life. He wants us to be satisfied. Psalm 128 describes how we can enter into these gracious, bountiful blessings of God by fearing Him and walking in His ways. As we do, we will be happy and it will be well with us. As the New Living translation renders it, "how rich your life." In this chapter, we will learn how we can experience the rich life God wants to give us.

In 2 Corinthians 8 and 9 Paul encouraged the church at Corinth to give a generous offering for the poor saints at Jerusalem. After he exhorted them to give bountifully and cheerfully in 2 Corinthians 9:6–7, he told them in verse 8 what God would do for them. He gave them a promise that not only applied to them but continues to be true for us today. If we will be tithers and givers, if we will give bountifully and cheerfully, God will make all grace abound toward us so that we will have sufficiency in all things and abound in every good work.

The key phrase in this verse is "all grace." God has the ability to make all grace abound toward us, and He will do this when we give bountifully and cheerfully. Our obedience to God puts Him in a position where He can make His grace abound toward us. The word "abound" means to superabound. God is able to give us all grace like we would throw a bounce pass. He can make His grace bounce toward us with such abundance that it overwhelms us and knocks us down. And He gives us all grace so that we might have "all sufficiency in all things." This is God's will for us.

How does God want us, His children who honor Jesus as Lord, to live? What kind of life does He want us to have? God wants us to be in a position where we always have and never lack. He does not want us to be in a place of blessing only temporarily and then fall out of it. Many Christians live from crisis to crisis. When something bad happens, they come to

God and receive from Him. Then they stop seeking Him and something bad happens again. They return to God and receive from Him again. Thus, the cycle of lack, no lack, and a return to lack continues.

However, God's will, as Proverbs 19:23 says, is that we abide satisfied. Similarly, Isaiah 26:3 says that God will keep us in perfect peace—*shalom shalom*—a position where we lack nothing and have all sufficiency. The Greek word that is translated "sufficiency" means self-satisfaction, contentment. God want us to be always satisfied. To be satisfied does not mean that we have just enough to make it. No, it means to be satiated, filled up. When we eat a large meal and have no desire to eat any more, our hunger is satisfied. God's will is that we reach the place where we are always satisfied.

Job 36:11 teaches that if we obey and serve Him we will spend our days in prosperity and our years in pleasures. Psalm 23 says that the Lord is our shepherd and we shall not lack. It adds that goodness and mercy will follow us all the days of our lives and promises that God will prepare a table before us in the presence of our enemies. Our cup will run over. Yes, God will bless us when we get to heaven, but we do not have to wait until heaven to enjoy it. We can have heaven on earth and then go to heaven and enjoy what our Lord has for us there too. He wants us to be always satisfied.

God has not failed to repeat His desire for us to be satisfied. In Psalm 91:16 He says, "With long life will I satisfy him." Again, in Jeremiah 31:14 He declares, "And I will satiate the soul of the priests with fatness, and my people shall be satisfied with my goodness." Deuteronomy 33:23 and Psalm 36:8 also testify to God's will for us to be satisfied. Yes, God is the same now as he has always been and always will be. His will for man has not changed and it will not change. He graciously provides us with a satisfying benefits package:

> Bless the LORD, O my soul, and forget not all his benefits: Who forgiveth all thine iniquities; who healeth all thy diseases; Who redeemeth thy life from destruction; who crowneth thee with lovingkindness and tender mercies; Who satisfieth thy mouth with good things."
>
> —Psalm 103:2–5

God says He will keep giving you His good things until you are satisfied. And even then, He is really not done. The Bible talks about us having so much that we do not have room enough to contain it: "good measure, pressed down, and shaken together, and running over" (Luke 6:38)

Both 2 Corinthians 8 and 9 and Philippians 4 talk about offering financial and material gifts for the kingdom of God. Therefore, when we read that God says He meets all our needs (Phil. 4:19) and causes us to always have all sufficiency in all things (2 Cor. 9:8), we tend to think only in financial terms. However, both of these scriptures refer to more than God blessing us with money. Thank God that it is His will for us to prosper financially and have wealth. However, we could have money and still not be satisfied. What good is being wealthy if we are sick or our marriage and family relationships are troubled? What good is having money if we lack in other areas of our lives?

God has provided for us so that we can have wealth, but wealth is really the lowest form of prosperity. He has made it possible for us to have not just wealth but also health, protection, wonderful marriages, and wonderful children. Really,

He wants us to prosper in every area of life. His will is that you always have all self-satisfaction, that you be satisfied in all things. If there is an area of your life where you are lacking, He wants to fill it up. He wants to fill you with such good things that you are satisfied.

Enriched to Show God's Greatness

Second Corinthians 9:11 sums up God's blessings with this phrase—being enriched. Do you notice the word in the middle of "enriched?" It is the will of God that we be rich, not just financially but in every area of life. God wants us to be rich in our marriages, our relationships with our children and our friends, our careers, our minds, and our bodies. He loves us, and His will is that we, His children, be blessed. What father would not want to see his children blessed? And His love for us far surpasses the love of an earthly father.

But God's love is not the only reason He wants to bless us so richly. He also wants to show the greatness of His grace so the world will look at us and say, "How rich your life is." This is what Jesus did in John 11 when He raised His friend Lazarus from the dead. Lazarus had been dead four days by the time Jesus came to the tomb where he was buried. After the stone was rolled away, He prayed to aloud to the Father, "I thank you that you have heard me." Then He yelled out, "Lazarus, come forth!" Lazarus came out alive, still bound in grave clothes, and Jesus said, "Loose him, and let him go."

As a result of this miracle, many of the Jews put their faith in Jesus (John 11:45). When He returned to Bethany six days before the Passover celebration, the people were very aware that Jesus was there. John 12:9 says that "they came not for Jesus' sake only, but that they might see Lazarus also, whom he had raised from the dead." The people wanted to see Jesus, but they also wanted to see the miracle work He had done. They wanted to see for themselves the man God had raised from the dead.

The chief priests responded to this interest in Jesus and Lazarus by talking about the idea of putting Lazarus to death (John 12:10). They had already decided that they wanted to kill Jesus, and now they wanted to include Lazarus. It was an expression of the hatred that the world has against Jesus and also those who follow Him. And their strong response against Lazarus showed that the resurrection miracle had made his life a testimony to the greatness and the goodness of God.

The people responded not only to Jesus preaching a message or performing the miracles of healing, deliverance, or resurrection. No, Lazarus' life—the fact that he was dead and Jesus had raised him from the dead—attracted their attention. Because of this, people received Jesus. And today, two thousand years later, God wants each of us to be a Lazarus to our world. He wants those around us to see that maybe we were dead financially but God gave us life. Maybe we were dead physically, but God has resurrected us and now we are healed. Or maybe our marriage relationship was on the rocks, but God resurrected it and now we are ravished with love.

God wants the world to look at our lives and see that He has blessed us. He wants our family and friends to come to Jesus not necessarily because they heard a great message, but because of what they have seen God do in us and for us. He wants those around us to come to the place where they look at our lives and say, "How rich your life is! Tell me how you got there." Then we can tell them about the King of Kings and the Lord of Lords, the one who is the Way, the Truth, and the Light, the one who is the resurrection himself. God is raising up Lazaruses wherever His children live, and many of us can already say, "That's me."

However, God has more work to do in some of us. God has given us a rich, abundant life, and that is a good confession. In fact, we may be dead at the same time we shout and run and say, "Glory to God! I am a Lazarus to the world." It is not good enough to only hear the good news of God's blessings; we also have to receive the gifts that flow from His grace. James 1:22 exhorts us, "But be ye doers of the word, and not hearers only." And just a few verses later, James 1:25 adds that the person who does the Word is the one who will be blessed in his deed. We must enter into the rich, abundant life of God's grace.

This is what Moses desired when he sent twelve spies to explore the Promised Land in Numbers 13. Moses told them, "Go and look at the land God is giving you, then come back and tell everybody how good it is." Today, God has blessed some of us so abundantly and He has given us a chance to explore our "promised land." As we discover the grapes of God's goodness, we can testify, "Look at these grapes! It is good in the land of God's grace!" We can tell others, "God has this for you, and here is the road to get there."

All Grace: The Key to All Sufficiency

"All grace," as 2 Corinthians 9:8 calls it, is the means through which we come to have all sufficiency and are satisfied in every area. It is the root that produces fruit in our lives. The Amplified Bible renders the phrase *all grace* as "every favor and earthly blessing." God's grace is not limited to only one or two blessings.

The word *grace* has many different meanings in Scripture, and we have to look at the context to know which meaning applies. In 2 Corinthians 9:8 it refers to God's anointing, or God's power. The fact that the apostle Paul said *all* grace testifies that God is all powerful. He has all the power He needs to meet whatever needs we have. Just as a lake empties into streams that water the areas where they go, God's glory—His presence and all his assets—empties into the streams of His graces or riches.

For example, He gives the grace that brings healing, the aspect of God's power that heals a sick body. He also gives the grace that brings wealth, "The blessing of the Lord" (Prov. 10:22) that "maketh rich." The word *rich* means to accumulate. When that anointing comes on us and we cooperate, it will cause us to be money magnets. Yet other streams of God's grace cause us to walk in divine protection or receive victory in times of trouble. Different graces are available for any need we have. It is all the power of God applied to different areas of our lives.

As we read the promise of 2 Corinthians 9:8, we tend to think that when we give money to him God will give money back to us. That is obviously true, as Luke 6:38 says, "Give and it shall be given unto you; good measure, pressed down, and shaken together, and running over." When we give to God our money is seed and He will give us a harvest of money. However, the power to get wealth is not all that God has provided for us when we give. That is only one stream. No, God promises to give you all grace. Your seed can meet any need because He wants you to be in a position where you always have all sufficiency in all things and are rich in every area."

I remember when Bishop Butler first shared the revelation that a seed will meet any need. As he taught it, he showed how people in the Bible gave financially and then received anointing that brought them healing, protection, victory, or whatever they needed. (This teaching is now included in the excellent book *A Seed Will Meet Any Need*.) However, I still could not understand how a seed would meet any need. While I was meditating on this, I received an audio tape of Dr. Creflo Dollar's message on the blessing of the Lord. It helped me understand that when we give to God, He pours out His anointing, His grace—the blessing—upon us. When we receive that blessing, we can act in faith and receive what we need.

God says that He will cause all grace to abound toward us. When we sow a seed God gives us grace—all grace, the blessing. When we give our tithes and offerings, we thank God for the privilege to minister to people through our giving. Then we say, "Father, we now receive the anointing. We receive the blessing right now by faith. We thank you that we have it." We may not receive money today or tomorrow, but we have released our faith to receive the anointing, the blessing, at that very moment.

We ask for our harvest and we believe that we receive it. God said He would give it, and He is faithful.

The Blessing of the Lord on Abraham and Sarah

Genesis 17 shows us what God makes available to us through the blessing that follows our giving. God promised Abram that he would have a son, even though he was 99 and his wife Sarai was 90. In verse 5, God renamed him Abraham, which means "the father of many nations." And in verse 15, God told Abraham, "As for Sarai thy wife, thou shalt not call her name Sarai, but Sarah shall her name be." Her new name simply meant "Princess," or "Mother of Nations." Abraham received these new names from God and declared with his mouth that he was the father of many nations and his wife was the mother of many nations. He called those things which be not as though they were (Rom. 4:17).

Saying what God says helps us believe what He has promised. If God says He will do something, we need to start speaking it aloud. We must stop talking defeat and start talking victory. If we talk defeat we will have defeat; however, if we talk victory we will have victory. This is why we must confess that we have a rich and abundant life. We must say, "Devil, I want you to hear this. No matter what you do, no matter what you say, I am living a rich and abundant life because my Daddy is rich in every way, and He has given me everything that belongs to Him."

After He gave Sarai the name Sarah, God told Abraham, "And I will bless her" (Gen. 17:16). In this verse, the word *bless* means "to endue with power for prosperity, success, fruitfulness, longevity, and more."[1] Zondervan comments on the word *blessed* and says, "In essence, the one who is blessed is given a rich and abundant life."[2] God was saying, "I am going to clothe Sarah with power, and this power, this blessing, will make her fruitful" (author's paraphrase). It is the same power that is available to us today.

We must remember that Sarah was ninety years old. She was not only barren, but she was also past the age of childbearing. Abraham was ninety-nine, and according to Romans 4:19, considered his body as good as dead. Is it any wonder that, according to Genesis 18:12, Sarah started laughing when she heard the Lord, in the form of a man, tell Abraham she would have a son?

But just as He said, God dropped His blessing on Sarah. He obviously dropped it on Abraham, too, because they did have a son in their old age. And after Sarah died at the age of 127, Abraham married again, and his second wife Keturah had six children. He received the blessing of the Lord, which makes us fruitful. God has made the same blessing available to born-again believers as they receive it by faith and call each other Daddy and Mommy, believing that He will produce the fruit of children.

The Blessing of the Lord for Our Health and Protection

And ye shall serve the LORD your God, and he shall bless thy bread, and thy water; and I will take sickness away from

the midst of thee. There shall nothing cast their young, nor
be barren, in thy land: the number of thy days I will fulfil.
—Exodus 23:25–26

God wants us to have all sufficiency in all things, and
this includes having a family that is healthy. As part of His
instructions for Israel in Exodus 23, He promised that if we
serve Him He will bless our food and drink. He speaks of
blessing that is an endowment, anointing, power on what we
eat. As we consider God's expression of care for our daily
sustenance, we need to do our part. We should obviously use
wisdom about where we eat. If a restaurant has a reputation
of being dirty, we should not eat there.

When we sit down to eat, we need to pray and thank God
for our food. How many people are without food, not only in
other nations but also here in the United States! Let us never
take for granted what God has done for us. It leads us into
mumbling and complaining, trouble and lack. And our prayer
over our food should not just be a ritual. We need to ask God
to put his blessing on our food and drink because it is our
own personal food and water purifier. When we ask that the
blessing be on our food, the anointing can come and cleanse
out anything that should not be in it. Our food will only be a
blessing to us.

The majority of our sicknesses are a result of the food we
eat. The number one disease in the country is heart disease,
and many times it is a direct result of what we have eaten. Many
times, cancer is also closely related to what we eat, although
it may also result from the household products we use. Many
health problems occur not because we ate something once, but

because we of our lifestyle of eating. If we sow a certain seed in our bodies again and again, it will produce corresponding fruit. But as we serve the Lord, He says that He will put His blessing on us and on our food. He will take sickness away from us.

As God continues to speak in Exodus 23, He promises that no one will have any miscarriages. He tells expectant mothers that He is going to put His blessing on you; He is going to cause His power to show up in your life, and it is going to cause your baby to be healthy, it is going to cause your baby to come at the right time. And then He goes on to say that He is going to give you long life, a long and healthy life.

All this comes to us by the power of God. He wants us to have a rich life, so he has made the blessing available to us. When we receive it and activate it by faith, our food is cleansed and we can walk in health. As we have mentioned, we typically think of the blessing as just money. However, it will also impact our bodies. It is not the will of God that we walk in any type of sickness or want. And His power to touch every part of our lives is still the same. It is available to us today.

In Deuteronomy 28 God gives Israel two lists, one that identifies the blessings for obedience and another that warns about the curses for disobedience. Verse 7 presents one of the blessings and says, "The LORD shall cause thine enemies that rise up against thee to be smitten before thy face: they shall come out against thee one way, and flee before thee seven ways." God says that He will beat down our foes before us. We may have multiple enemies who come as a unified force, confident and ready to fight, as the three nations that came against Judah in 2 Chronicles 20. However, because of the blessing they will be fleeing "seven ways," running all over the place when they leave.

God promises that He will protect us from anything Satan brings against us. As Isaiah 54:17 assures us, no weapon formed against us shall prosper. And Psalm 91:7 says that a thousand may fall by your side and ten thousand by your right hand, but it will not come near you. The blessing of the Lord will act like a force field, and believers who have to go into physical danger in the place of war can step out with faith in God's care. We see this in Genesis 14, where Abraham, with God's blessing on him, took 318 trained servants and chased four armies, defeating them in battle. The blessing was on David when he killed Goliath. And Leviticus 26:8 says, "And five of you shall chase an hundred, and an hundred of you shall put ten thousand to flight."

Judges 13–16 tells the story of Samson and the success he experienced against the Philistines because the blessing was on him. The testimony of God's supernatural strength in his life was repeated a few years ago when someone broke into the home of an elderly woman in Detroit. This woman, who was small and about ninety years old, literally said, "Lord, I call on the power of Samson." In the moments that followed, she overpowered the intruder and he was arrested. He had to be the most embarrassed man in the city of Detroit. It was evident that the blessing of the Lord was upon her. And it is available to us, too.

Three Keys to Receiving the Blessing

And Joseph was brought down to Egypt; and Potiphar, an officer of Pharaoh, captain of the guard, an Egyptian, bought him of the hands of the Ishmaelites, which had brought him down thither. And the LORD was with Joseph, and he was a prosperous man; and he was in the house of his master the Egyptian. And his master saw that the LORD was with him, and that the LORD made all that he did to prosper in his hand. And Joseph found grace in his sight, and he served him: and he made him overseer over his house, and all that he had he put into his hand. And it came to pass from the time that he had made him overseer in his house, and over all that he had, that the LORD blessed the Egyptian's house for Joseph's sake and the blessing of the LORD was upon all that he had in the house, and in the field.

—Genesis 39:1–5

Joseph's life is a powerful example of one who has the blessing of the Lord. Even though he was a slave, he had the anointing to prosper. As he went about his work, the blessing of God came on him, and he had extraordinary success. His master, Potiphar, recognized that the Lord was with him. Because of this, Joseph found grace—favor—with Potiphar, and became his personal assistant, the overseer of his house. Because the blessing was on Joseph, it was also over Potiphar's house and fields. God gave increase not only to Joseph, but also to his master and the household he served.

The story of Joseph's success teaches what Deuteronomy 28

says, which is that God will cause the blessing to manifest in our lives, in everything we put our hands to do (Deut. 28:8). We should be the best at our work, whatever it may be, because we have the anointing of the Lord available to us. As the blessing is manifested in our lives, God will give us favor with people who will open doors of opportunity for us. He will give us favor where we work and with our employers who happen to be heathens.

The blessing that was upon Joseph can be ours as we use three keys:

- **Bring God all the tithes**—When we do this, He promises to open the windows of heaven and pour out His blessing (Mal. 3:10). We have to tithe to receive the blessing, the anointing, the grace described in 2 Corinthians 9:8. This is the minimum God requires. In 2 Corinthians 9 He speaks to us about giving above our tithes.

- **Sow seed**—The Christians at Philippi gave offerings to provide financial support for Paul. They sowed seed to help the kingdom of God expand. In response to this, Paul told them that because of their gifts "my God shall supply all your need according to his riches in glory" (Phil. 4:19). Do you notice that he did not say "all your financial need." No he said "*all* your need." And the provision would come according to God's riches—His anointing—in glory. We must follow the example of the Philippians and sow seed for the growth of the kingdom of God.

- **Give to the poor**—This actually falls under the category of sowing seed, but I believe it is important to highlight. God cares about the poor, and this became very evident to me when I did a search and found 199 scriptures about them. If we call ourselves people of God we should care about the poor as much as He does. In 2 Corinthians 9, Paul was asking people to give to *poor* saints. We must give to the poor. And when we do, we give a blessing.

Receiving and using these keys will enable us to enjoy the blessing of the Lord. We can release our faith for whatever we need and we will find that a seed will indeed meet any need. We will be able to say, "How rich my life is!"

Chapter 11

MANIFESTING GOD'S PRESENCE

*Yet a little while, and the world seeth me no more;
but ye see me: because I live, ye shall live also. At
that day ye shall know that I am in my Father,
and ye in me, and I in you. He that hath my
commandments, and keepeth them, he it is that
loveth me: and he that loveth me shall be loved of
my Father, and I will love him, and will manifest
myself to him. Judas saith unto him, not Iscariot,
"Lord, how is it that thou will manifest thyself to
us, and not to the world?" Jesus answered and
said unto him, If a man love me, he will keep my
words: and my Father will love him, and we will
come unto him and make our abode with him.*
—John 14:19–23

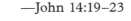

JESUS GAVE THIS promise to His disciples the night before His death. As we noted in chapter 5, it is for all who live in "that day," (John 14:20), the day we live in now since Christ's death and resurrection. It is for us today and expresses God's will that we keep His commandments.

The word *commandment* means authoritative prescription or injunction. We as believers need to make sure that we have God's commandments—His orders—and we can do this by spending time in His Word on a consistent basis. It is also important that we keep His commandments. In John 14:15 Jesus said, "If you love me, keep my commandments." The word *keep* has a deeper meaning than doing God's commandments. It means to guard by keeping the eye upon, to fulfill a command, to maintain.

Jesus wants us to keep our eyes on His commandments and consistently do them. He instructs us to maintain a lifestyle of doing God's commandments. Jesus did not say, "The one who received me as Lord and Savior, he is the one who loves me." No, He said, "He who has my commandments and maintains a lifestyle of doing them is the one who loves me" (author's paraphrase). If we love God, we will show it by our actions. We will keep his commandments. We may say, "I love you, Lord. I exalt you, Lord." However, if we are not keeping his commandments we are lying to Him.

God gave us his commandments for two important reasons. First, he gave them to us because they keep us in the path of blessing and life. If we do God's commandments, He can bless us abundantly. Obedience brings blessing, and blessing brings prosperity. And, of course, Psalm 35:27 says that God takes pleasure in the prosperity of His servant. He enjoys it when we are prospering. He likes to watch us be blessed.

The second reason God gave us His commandments was to instruct us to bless others. He wants us to be a blessing through giving, praying, witnessing, or any other action He calls us to do. And, of course, God is blessed when other people are blessed. He takes pleasure in their prosperity, particularly when our witness helps them become a part of God's family. There is no greater blessing to God.

If we love God, we will understand the importance of knowing and keeping His commandments. We will say, "Since I love you, God, I am going to keep your commandments. I want you to enjoy watching the blessings that follow my obedience." And as we keep God's commandments, we will be loved by Him. He says that the one who keeps His commandments is a person who loves Him, and He will be a friend to him; He has affection for him, and He will attach Himself to him.

John 3:16 teaches that God loved the world so much that He gave His only begotten son to provide salvation and eternal life for every person. He sent His Son to earth to die for every man, woman, and child and give all of us the opportunity to become part of His family. This is the God kind of love, *agape*, as it is called in Greek. It encompasses *phileo* love, which means "to be a friend to, to be fond of an individual or an object, to have affection for," denoting personal attachment, tender affection. *Vines Expository Dictionary* explains that both these apply to Jesus' words, "he that loveth me shall be loved of my Father."[1]

In Deuteronomy 7:12–13 God gave a similar promise to Israel: If they would keep His commandments, then He would keep His covenant with them. His covenant was to love, bless, and multiply His people. As we learned about *phileo* love, the Hebrew word for "love" also means to have affection for. An affectionate parent will hug his child. God is more loving than the most affectionate parent, and He says that when we keep His commandments, when we show that we love Him, He can come and put His arms around us. He can attach Himself to us. He is affectionate towards us.

God says that He will not only love us, but He will also bless us. He is affectionate toward us and fond of us. We have favor with Him. And beyond that, He will multiply and increase us. This is what happens when we have God's commandments and keep them and "are loved of [the] Father." I like the idea of God being my best friend who is fond of me. I enjoy having favor with Him.

But Jesus desires something more than a relationship of love and blessing. He also wants to manifest Himself to us. The word *manifest* means to exhibit in person, to be in a position of being seen. When we talk about manifestation of healing we mean that it actually shows up in our bodies. The manifestation of financial harvest is money actually coming into our hands. The manifestation of divine protection is an actual instance of God shielding us from something that comes against us. Something that is manifested is actually exhibited, it is shown. In John 14:21 Jesus promises to manifest Himself and exhibit Himself to him who is loved of the Father."

The Manifest Presence of God

What does it mean for Jesus to manifest Himself in our lives? Second Chronicles 16:9 says that "the eyes of the LORD run to and fro throughout the whole earth, to shew himself strong in the behalf of them whose heart is perfect toward him." God steps into the middle of our needs and shows off. When God shows up, He is going to show off. Jesus tells us that if you love Him, the Father will love you, and He will step in. He will manifest Himself on your behalf.

This is Jesus' promise to us: He will show up in your life, your mind, your body, your emotions, your finances, your marriage, and your relationship with your children. He will show up on your job, and He will show up by giving you protection and wisdom. If you love Him He will show up in your life. Whenever you need Him, He will come." As He said in John 15:7: "If ye abide in me, and my words abide in you, ye shall ask what ye will, and it shall be done unto you."

As we consider Jesus' love and His plan to manifest Himself in our lives, we notice the question the apostle Judas (not Iscariot) asked Him. Judas responded to Jesus' statement from a natural viewpoint. Perhaps he thought Jesus was saying that He would walk through the wall to be with them. How could he do that without anyone else seeing Him?

Jesus' reply gives us another nugget about His will, another part of His promise. He says that if you love Him, you will keep His words and His Father will love you. Together they will come to you and show up in your life. They will exhibit Themselves. They will show Themselves strong in your behalf." The word *come* means to appear, to accompany. Jesus was expressing the truth that He and the Father will manifest themselves in us. Then He went a step farther and said that He and the Father will also make their abode—take up residence—with us.

"If you love me," Jesus was saying, "My Father and I are going to manifest ourselves in your life. But when we show up, we are not going anywhere. We are not just coming to visit; we are going to stay with you. We will walk with you and talk with you, and we will be next to you when you sleep and when you wake up. We will be alongside you when you go to work and when you are with your children. We will be with you in everything you do. Whenever you need us to step in and do something, We are with you, ready to bring it to pass."

This is so much more than Jesus showing up when we need Him. It means that He manifests Himself in everything, and, as a result, we will prosper in every arena of life. Because God is with us all the time, his manifest presence is on us. We will prosper in our families, our bodies, our finances, and on our jobs. We will experience what Psalm 34:15 means when it says that "the eyes of the Lord are upon the righteous, and his ears are open unto their cry." God is near to the righteous, and He hears their prayers. This is the will of God for us, and we can enjoy it by loving Jesus and keeping His commandments."

However, if we do not receive and obey Christ's words, He is not walking with us. He will not leave us per se, but He cannot be with us or next to us. He does not have access to step in and do what He needs to do. Those who are not righteous, those who are not living right, cannot enjoy the manifest presence of God. In fact, Psalm 34:16 says that His face "is against them that do evil." If we disobey God's commandments, we cannot claim Jesus and then expect Him to be with us ready to answer our prayers.

The manifest presence of God, which might also be called "the blessing of the Lord," was on Abraham. Genesis 24:1 says, "And Abraham was old...and the LORD had blessed Abraham in all things." It was also on his great-grandson Joseph, for, as Genesis 39:2, 21, and 23 testify, "the Lord was with him." Joseph's brothers sold him into slavery, but the manifest presence of God caused him to prosper so that he became the number one servant in his master's house. After his master's wife falsely accused him of sexual wrongdoing, he was thrown into prison. But again the Lord was with him, and he rose to the position of head prisoner.

In God's appointed time, He opened a door for Joseph to come into Pharaoh's presence. Because the Lord was with him, Joseph was able to interpret Pharaoh's dreams. God exalted him to be second only to Pharaoh and gave him wisdom to help Egypt prepare for the seven years of famine that would follow the seven years of plenty. Egypt followed Joseph's leadership and saved 20 percent of the food from the produce of the good years. Egypt had food for its people and also for everyone who came from other lands that were suffering from the famine. Joseph prospered in his job, and Egypt also prospered under his leadership.

Joseph went from lead slave to prime minister of Egypt, all because the Lord was with him. The manifest presence of God was on his life. God wants each of us to also live with God's manifest presence on us. No matter where we go or what is happening, God is with us in every area of our lives. He is producing for us. It is part of our destiny, part of what Jesus paid for when He died and rose again. But there is a key to manifesting God's presence, and it is loving one another.

The Key of Loving One Another

And whatsoever we ask, we receive of him, because we keep his commandments, and do those things that are

pleasing in his sight. And this is his commandment, That
we should believe on the name of his Son Jesus Christ, and
love one another, as he gave us commandment.

—1 John 3:22–23

Loving one another is not optional. Jesus said that if you
love Him, you will keep His commandment. If we are not
obeying His commandment to love one another, we do not
really love Jesus. Loving one another is key to manifesting God
in our lives. We want God to show up in our situations, but we
must remember Galatians 5:6, which says that faith works by
love. If faith is the car, love is the gas; and we all know that a
car does not go anywhere without gas.

This is so important. We need faith to manifest God in our
lives, and this means that we have to truly love one another, not
just when others do good, but also when they do wrong and
say what they should not say. The love God commands is not
moved by emotions. It is a commitment, a choice we make in
the human will. It means that we look at someone who offends
us and mean it when we say, "I love you." This is what God
requires of us.

In John 14:23 Jesus said that those who love Him keep His
commandments. This is what we must do if we desire to have
God's presence manifested in our lives. And what are God's
commandments? They can all be summed up in one commandment: "Believe on the name of his Son Jesus Christ, and love
one another, as he gave us commandment" (1 John 3:23). If we
do this one commandment, we will have done them all. Sometimes we get caught up in the do's and don'ts and what we
should or should not be doing. However, all we really need to

do is obey this one commandment. If we do, God's will for our daily attitudes and actions will be clear.

The first part of God's commandment is that we should "believe on the name of His Son Jesus Christ." God tells us to receive Jesus Christ as Lord of our lives. Jesus went around preaching that the Kingdom of God is at hand, calling the people to repent and believe. God's command to the world has not changed. It is still, "Repent and believe." This is the gospel, which God calls us to obey. If we do not obey the gospel, we put ourselves in position to go to hell when we die. And, of course, we face suffering in this life too.

God commands us to believe. Hebrews 10:38 quotes from Habakkuk 2:4 and says, "Now the just shall live by faith: but if any man draw back, my soul shall have no pleasure in him." God speaks to all who are not born again, and commands them to believe. If a person disobeys this command, he is robbed of God's blessings here on earth and loses the gift of eternal life in heaven. In John 14:6 Jesus said, "I am the way, the truth, and the life: no man cometh unto the Father, but by me." We do not come by good works or by the many religious leaders whose lives and teachings deny Christ and biblical truth. The God of the Bible makes it clear that you have to believe on the name of God's Son Jesus Christ because He is the one who came and died and rose again for your salvation.

The second part of that same commandment is that we should "love one another, as he gave us commandment." In John 13:34, Jesus commanded us to "love one another; as I have loved you." We are to love our fellow believers, as 1 John 3:18 explains, "in deed and in truth." The word "truth" means sincerity. We must ask ourselves if we truly love our brother or just put up with him. We should not just say we love, but truly love and act like it.

First Peter 4:8 says, "And above all things have fervent charity among yourselves." Peter told us to have not just love, but *fervent* love—energetic love, white-hot love—for each other. This is love that expresses joy in our brothers and sisters in Christ. The apostle Paul communicated it to the church at Philippi when he addressed them as "my brethren dearly beloved and longed for, my joy and crown" (Phil. 4:1). We need to have this genuine love inside us before it will show on the outside.

We in the United States have a very individualistic society. On the other hand, many other nations are group-oriented and think in terms of "we" and "us." Both of these cultural approaches have good and bad parts, but the kingdom culture has the best of both. Yes, I have to do what God has called me to do. I need to step up and be diligent. I need to have a vision and focus for my life. But I also need to have an "us" mentality. This is my family and I love every single person in it. It is not just that I love my wife and my children, or I love my husband, or I love my brother and sister. No, I also love my brother and sister in Christ.

God is telling us to love one another like we love our natural siblings. If we say we cannot, we are lying. God would not command it if we could not make the decision. Love is first a decision. The first part of keeping His commandment to love Him is choosing to truly love each other.

The apostle John takes us a step farther in our understanding of God's command to love one another in 1 John 5:1, "Whosoever believeth that Jesus is the Christ is born of God: and every one that loveth him that begat loveth him also that is begotten of him." This verse teaches us that if we love God, we will also love our brothers and sisters in Christ. If someone chooses to receive Jesus through faith that He is the Messiah, the Son of God, he is born again. He is born of God, and God is his Father. Therefore, if we love the God, who "begat" (gave birth) to the believer, we will also love the believer.

First John 4:20–21 presents a clear picture of how necessary it is for us to love one another:

> If a man say, I love God, and hateth his brother, he is a liar: for he that loveth not his brother whom he hath seen, how can he love God whom he hath not seen? And this commandment have we from him, That he who loveth God loveth his brother also.

This is a strong warning that we cannot hate our brother and say that we love God. We cannot hold a grudge against someone and say that we love God. If we have to go to the other side of the church to avoid someone, how can we say that we love God? If we do not love our brother, who we have physically seen, how can we love God whom we have not seen? Love does not keep a grudge. If we have love for our brothers and sisters in Christ, we cannot look at one of them and believe the worst of him. We must guard against judging other believers, and this includes new Christians who may become easily discouraged in the infancy of their faith.

Love That Fulfills the Law

> For for this cause, pay ye tribute also: for they are God's ministers, attending continually upon this very thing.

Render therefore to all their dues: tribute to whom tribute is due, custom to whom custom; fear to whom fear; honour to whom honour. Owe no man any thing, but to love one another: for he that loveth another hath fulfilled the law. For this, Thou shalt not commit adultery, Thou shalt not kill, Thou shalt not steal, Thou shalt not bear false witness, Thou shalt not covet; and if there be any other commandment, it is briefly comprehended in this saying, namely, Thou shalt love thy neighbour as thyself. Love worketh no ill to his neighbour: therefore love is the fulfilling of the law.

—Romans 13:6–10

In Romans 13, the apostle Paul told the Christians in Rome to be subject to those in places of governmental authority. He explained that God has placed rulers over us to punish those who do wrong and that we are to obey them as a matter of conscience. As he talked about this, he also said that we are to pay taxes to support the work of those who are "God's ministers" to provide protection for us. These people would include police officers, soldiers, and many others who serve us.

Paul taught us that we should not evade taxes. We should not owe anything but love to the people God has placed in our lives, and this includes people in positions of authority. We are commanded to not just love other Christians, but to also love the sinner and even our enemies. It is one thing to love our brothers and sisters in Christ. However, it is another thing to love the difficult person who lives next door so much that you will go after his soul. Lack of genuine love for the lost has been the reason we do not win souls. We do not truly care about them, but only about ourselves.

If we love other believers and love sinners, we fulfill the Law. The Hebrew word for "law" is *Torah*, which simply means God's teachings and instruction. It refers, of course, to the Old Testament Law, which we find in Exodus, Leviticus, Numbers, and Deuteronomy. If we truly love, we are doing everything in God's law.

But what does "love" mean? How do we live it in our daily lives? Love acts a certain way. It will do things that honor God, but it will absolutely refuse to do things that dishonor Him. Paul identified some of the things that love will not do:

- **"Thou shalt not commit adultery"**—To sleep with another man's wife is surely not operating in love to either the other man or to his wife. First Corinthians 6 says that one who commits sexual sin has sinned against his own body. He has also helped another person to do the same. Love does not do this.

- **"Thou shalt not kill"**—The Hebrew word for "kill" means murder, and it is obvious that one who murders someone is not showing love. This command does not necessarily forbid war. God sent the people of Israel to war and told them to wipe out the Canaanites as instruments of His judgment upon them. However, it does forbid the murder of all people, both outside the womb and in the womb. To kill an unborn child is to deny that person a chance to live and fulfill the call of God for him here on earth. God will forgive the murder of the unborn child, but we must warn against it when we talk to people who are facing that decision.

- **"Thou shalt not steal"**—It is very clear that stealing from someone is not an act of love. You are bringing harm to their life.

- **"Thou shalt not bear false witness"**—To bear false witness is to lie, and this is not a practice of love. Once again, you are bringing harm to them.

- **"Thou shalt not covet"**—At first glance, we might think that desiring what someone has would not hurt them. However, James 3:16 says that "where envying and strife is, there is confusion and every evil work." Coveting will harm the other person, and it is not a work of love.

These are five of the Ten Commandments found in Exodus 20:1–17, and they tell us in negative terms how to love others. (A sixth commandment gives the positive instruction, "Honor thy father and mother." The other four commandments—the first four in the Bible listing—teach us how to relate to God.). But as Paul came to the end of them, he introduced another commandment, one that encompasses any other commandment there might be: love your neighbor as yourself.

Who is our neighbor? A lawyer asked Jesus this question in Luke 10:29, and in the verses that followed, Jesus answered him with the story of the Good Samaritan. A Jewish man going from Jerusalem to Jericho was beaten and robbed and left for dead on the side of the road. The man who helped him was a

Samaritan, a person from a mixed race that had resulted from the intermarriage of Jews and foreigners. Jesus basically said that our neighbor is anyone God wants us to touch with His love. It does not matter who they are or what is going on in their life. People who suffer from natural disasters in other parts of the world are our neighbors.

Love means that we will not injure or harm another physically, financially, or in any other way. We will not harm them with our attitudes, words or actions. Love works no ill, and it fulfills every command that God has given us. It is God's will for us, the key for God to manifest Himself in our lives.

The Actions of Love

Charity [love] suffereth long, and is kind; charity envieth not; charity vaunteth not itself, is not puffed up, Doth not behave itself unseemly, seeketh not her own, is not easily provoked, thinketh no evil; Rejoiceth not in iniquity, but rejoiceth in the truth; Beareth all things, believeth all things, hopeth all things, endureth all things. Charity never faileth.

—1 Corinthians 13:4–8

First Corinthians 13 begins by telling us that speaking in tongues, the gifts of the Spirit, all revelation, all faith, giving everything we have, and dying for a cause are worth nothing if we do not have love. The chapter concludes with the declaration that three things abide: faith, hope and love. Of these three, love is the greatest. Love is of God, and God is love (1 John 4:7–8). Because love is the greatest force on earth, we need to master it.

The middle verses of 1 Corinthians 13 give practical instruction on how to express what the Amplified Bible calls "God's love in us" (1 Cor. 13:5). They show us how to relate to others with the kind of love that does not cause ill to one's neighbor. And they identify the ways God manifests Himself through us. Let's take a look at the way love acts.

- **Love is longsuffering and kind.** Love will wait for a husband or wife to change for the better, and it will be kind in the process. It will sacrifice emotional desires while it waits for the resolution of problems in relationships with others.

- **Love does not envy.** Love does not envy what someone else has. Instead of envying another, we need to thank God for what He has given us. When we envy someone, we also speak wrongly about them and act badly toward them. Envy is accompanied by "every evil work" (James 3:16).

- **Love does not vaunt itself.** Love does not boast. Boasting puts oneself on a pedestal and injures others.

- **Love is not "puffed up."** Love does not operate in pride. It does not exult in stepping on others. love is humble.

- **Love does not behave in an unseemly way.** Love is not rude or, as the Amplified Bible says, "unmannerly." The word *unseemly* means unbecomingly. Love does not scream, curse, throw things, or talk critically about someone. Do not let your flesh have its way. Love does not do that.

- **Love does not seek her own.** Love is not selfish. Instead of always thinking about itself, it is selfless. It gives, and it realizes a greater blessing in giving than receiving. If life is centered only on *me* or *mine*, we are disobeying 1 Corinthians 10:24, which says, "Let no man seek his own, but every man another's." Love is helping another fulfill the vision God has given him as we trust God to fulfill His plans for us.

- **Love is not easily provoked.** Love is not easily exasperated. In the words of the Amplified Bible, it "is not touchy or fretful or resentful." If others have to walk on eggshells around us, we are not operating in love and we are harming others. Love has tough skin. It is not just going to react because someone said something that may have been hurtful. If someone says or does something that offends us, we are anchored in what God has said, and we can pray for them. We must grow into maturity in this area.

- **Love thinks no evil.** Love, according to the Amplified Bible, "is ever ready to believe the best of every person." It assumes the best of the intentions others have, and it sees them at their best. It also, according to the Amplified Bible, "takes no account of the evil done to it." Love does not keep a long list of offenses against it.

- **Love does not rejoice in iniquity, but in the truth.** Love does not rejoice in seeing people live wrong. It is not happy about unrighteousness or injustice because it understands that they lead to failure and poverty. On the other hand, love does want people to walk in truth because it leads to prosperity. Love likes to watch others prosper, not fail.

- **Love bears, believes, hopes, and endures all things.** Love is strong. It has endurance and stubbornly holds on.

- **Love never fails.** It is like the Energizer Bunny: it just keeps going and going. Our love for others should never run out. We should operate in love toward them at all times, in every situation. The word *fail* means "to be entirely idle (useless), to become of no effect." Love will always work when we are relating to others. It may not always appear to work right away, but if we truly love, it will work. It will reach into their hearts and allow God to step into their lives. It will allow God to change what needs to be changed if they are willing.

God wants to manifest Himself in our lives today. He will do it as we love our brothers and sisters in Christ and also as we love those who are lost. He commands us to love not only in word or in tongue, but in deed and in truth (1 John 3:18).

176

Chapter 12

PREPARING FOR THE GOOD DAYS

For he that will love life, and see good days, let him
refrain his tongue from evil, and his lips that they
speak no guile: Let him eschew evil, and do good;
let him seek peace, and ensue it.
—1 Peter 3:10–11

G OOD DAYS ARE coming." This was God's promise
to the people of Israel when, in Deuteronomy 8:7–9
and 28:1–14, He told them about the good land He was
going to give them and the blessings He would pour out
on them there. Joshua 21:43–45 records that God did
give them the land He had promised. He did bless them
abundantly. In fact, "There failed not ought of any good
thing which the LORD had spoken unto the house of
Israel; all came to pass" (Josh. 21:45).

God continues to promise good days for us. The
apostle Peter spoke confidently about God's provision of

good days in 1 Peter 3:10–11 and gave us instructions to enter into them. And the Spirit of God has been saying it through many who minister His Word today. God has made a lot of promises—in His Word and to us personally—and some of them have not come to pass yet. But we know that He is well able to keep His promises. He has done it before, and He will do it again.

The Bible records how the people of God have sometimes waited long periods of time for Him to keep His promises. Sometimes it did not look like any of the things He said were going to happen. However, every single promise He made came to pass. Yes, God is a perfectionist. He does not leave anything undone. If He said He will do something, He will do it. The days are here—right in front of us—when God is going to fulfill His promises. We are going to live out the days ahead with shouting and dancing and running! We are in the greatest times man has ever seen. It is time for the glory!

God wants us to have good days. Job 36:11 says that God wants us to spend our years in pleasures. Our bad days are over if we just receive what the Spirit of God is saying. We have to exchange our "worst case" scenario mentality for a "best case" scenario mentality. We need to stop thinking about negative things that have happened before and focus on what God has said. He wants us to have good days, not bad days, so that a sinner can look at our lives and say, "Boy you had a good day, what is going on?"

The will of God is that we love life and see good days. However, even though we are in the season for this, it is not going to happen automatically. We must receive and practice Peter's exhortation. Many Christians will take hold of it and live it out in the overflow of the Holy Spirit. Others will miss it. When Jesus rose from the dead, He appeared to his apostles. I cannot imagine a more spectacular, supernatural, joyous event. All of the eleven were there but Thomas. He missed the risen Christ that day, although in God's loving plan, he was able to come and see and receive at a later time.

In chapter 8, we discussed the parable of the sower in Mark 4:1–20 and saw that the Word produced fruit in only one of four groups who heard it. Was that God's will? No, it was because the people would not open their hearts to receive it. They would not do what was necessary to walk it out. We may struggle and go back and forth between really serving God and not serving Him. However, now is the time to forget about our past failures and give our lives to God. He is not a God of failure, but a God of success. Don't miss out. Good days are coming!

Guard Against Evil

How can we prepare for the good days ahead? What must we do to enjoy them?' First, we must refrain our tongues from evil and our lips from speaking guile. We must, as Ephesians 4:29 says, let no corrupt communication proceed from our mouths. It is so important that we keep our mouths from speaking ill of people and never use words to hurt them. We must practice this in our church fellowships.

We must also keep our mouths from speaking words of unbelief about our life situations. Such words are evil to God. If we come and release our faith for healing, we receive it. Even though we may not receive an instant manifestation of healing, we must guard against saying "Well, I did not get my healing." The Bible says believers shall lay hands on the sick and they shall recover (Mark 16:18). It teaches us about faith and tells us to pray and believe that we receive. When we do, we have what we desire (Mark 11:24). We may not have a physical manifestation immediately, but our healing is in the bank account.

It is evil to speak words of unbelief about things we have brought to God in faith. We must not allow the enemy to trick us into saying what he wants us to see in our situations. Instead, we must say what God says. The one who is hurting can say, "I am healed." Any who is in desperate financial need can say, "I am rich." And the person who is depressed can say, "I have joy like a river." If we say what God says, we will experience the overflow of His glory.

The weeks, the months, the years ahead are good days, and God will manifest His glory in our lives. Satan may have beaten up on us in the past, but things are going to change. God is going to pour out His blessings upon us in abundance. I am convinced that most people defeat themselves with the words they speak. They talk themselves out of their own blessings, instead of talking themselves into receiving God's gracious gifts. We must make a commitment that we will not speak negative words that rob us of the good things God has for us.

As we take steps to guard our mouths from speaking words of unbelief, we must be careful that we do not rehearse our problems over and over. It is one thing to tell our needs to people who can encourage our faith in God's provision. Indeed, they can pray with us. But other people do not need to know what we are facing. The more we talk about the negative, the worse we feel. If we talk about it long enough, what began as a little molehill will turn into a mountain. Instead of rehearsing our problems, we need to rehearse our victory—"This is what God is going to do for me." Some people may laugh at us, but in the end we will be laughing.

Second, we must "eschew evil". The word *eschew* means to escape, get away from. Proverbs 4:27 warns, "Turn not to the right hand nor to the left: remove thy foot from evil." And Proverbs 8:13 says, "The fear of the Lord is to hate evil." When the Word of God talks about evil, it teaches us not to get next to it. It is obvious that we will not see good days if we give ourselves to evil. Sin produces bad days.

We must be careful about entering what I call the "temptation zone." Many believers live their lives in this zone. They get as close as they can to sin and then fight like mad to not commit it. They do not want to sin in their heart, but their flesh does. For example, a man and a woman who are dating need to commit themselves to glorify God in their bodies. When they do, they must avoid activities that will foster the temptation of sexual sin. If the do not, they will find it very difficult to remain pure. First Corinthians 6:18 says, "Flee fornication." The Bible not only forbids sin; it also teaches us to hate sin and not even get near it.

The enemy has established the temptation zone in many areas of life. Some Christians believe that it is all right to sip a little wine. Others say, "Well, beer is okay, but wine is not." I wonder why we just cannot give it up if we love God. Proverbs 20:1 warns, "Wine is a mocker, strong drink is raging: and whosoever is deceived thereby is not wise." And then there is the temptation zone of movies that influence us to evil. If we know that the plot or pictures of a movie will turn our thoughts or entice our flesh to sin, we must stay away from it.

Relationships can lead us into the temptation zone. A new Christian may want to hang out with his old friends who are not saved. But is he influencing them toward Christ, or are they influencing him away from his faith in Christ? And a born-again, Spirit-filled sister may gossip about someone or complain about something at church when she meets with her Christian friends. We must remove ourselves from these kinds of temptation so that we do not sin.

And we must also beware of the temptation zone around internet pornography, an industry that makes more money than all four major sports combined. To the shame of Christians, not all that money comes from sinners. Internet pornography gives us the opportunity to sin in the privacy of our bedroom, living room, or work office. We need to do whatever is necessary to build high walls around this temptation to evil.

Do Good and Seek Peace

Good days are coming as we choose to guard against evil in our speech and our actions. As we obey God in these areas, we must also do good. When we received Jesus we became new creatures. God could have taken us home to heaven immediately, but He left us here because He has a job for us to do. He has given us a purpose, a mission to make disciples for him. God has placed us in the cities where we live and the jobs where we work so we can fulfill our part of this mission there.

Ephesians 4:11–12 teaches that Christ gave the ministry gifts, which include pastors, to help prepare us to do the work of the ministry He has called us to do. When we come to church, we receive the ministry of God's Word to equip us for our part in God's work. Second Timothy 3:16–17 says that all Scripture is God-breathed and tells that it is profitable for doctrine, reproof, correction, and instruction in righteousness so that we may become spiritually mature and thoroughly prepared to do all good works.

We must do good for God to receive good from God. And what is the good work He wants us to do? First, it is soul winning. Some people think that soul winning is the pastor's job. No, his job is to train believers so they can go and do it. What would happen if every Christian won one person to Christ every month? O, how the church would grow!

Discipling new believers is another good work. When we win a person to Christ, we must bring him to church to help him grow in his newfound faith. We must not leave him alone without spiritual encouragement. The Bible introduces us to other good works—healing, giving, and praying for other people. All these good works are God's purpose for us. If we want to see good days, we have to do good works.

Finally, God commands us to seek peace. Hebrews 12:14 instructs us to "follow peace with all men." Romans 12 says to live peaceably with all men. Ephesians 4:3 instructs us to endeavor to keep the bond of peace. The way we accomplish these commands is walking in love with others.

Get Ready!

Yes, good days are coming. God wants us to enter into the blessings of these days, and He has told us how to prepare for them: watch your mouth, stay away from evil; do good for God, and seek peace. God wants us to be happy, as a result of the good things we receive from Him. In John 16:24, Jesus promised, "Ask, and ye shall receive, that your joy may be full." In John 15:7, He also said, "If ye abide in me, and my words abide in you, ye shall ask what ye will, and it shall be done unto you." We can ask God for whatever we want and He will give us good things so that our joy may be full.

We might say that good days are already here. Proverbs 4:18 says, "But the path of the just is as the shining light, that shineth more and more unto the perfect day." We, as God's children, are walking on this path. Every step we take is brighter, with more glory, just as the sun increases to the fullness of its daytime glory. But even though we are enjoying glory right now, the sun is not yet at its highest point. The goodness we have received from God is wonderful, but it can get better!

In one respect, we cannot wait to go to heaven because it is better than anything on this planet. Some may want to go to heaven right now because they cannot stand their life today. But this is not God's will. Instead, He wants us to love life and see good days here. He wants to satisfy us with long life, like Abraham, who, when he was old, was blessed in all things (Gen. 24:1). God wants to bless us in every part of our lives so the world will see that what He has done. He wants to use us to change the lives of those around us.

Ephesians 2:7 says that in the ages to come God is going

to show us the riches of his kindness toward us. He is going to surprise us with ages' worth of good things. Our spiritual destiny, not only on this earth, but for eternity, is to go from glory to glory. As we walk on the stairway to glory, we know that God always outdoes himself. He provides all that we need to live life to the full. Good days *are* coming! Get ready!

NOTES

Chapter 4
Entering Into Wellness

1. *Bible in Basic English* (Cambridge, England: Cambridge University Press, 1982).

Chapter 9
Walking in Humility

1. W. E. Vine, *Vine's Expository Dictionary of Old and New Testament Words* (Nashville, TN: Nelson, 1997), s.v. "humility."

Chapter 10
Enjoying a Rich Life

1. Gleason Archer, R. Laird Harris, and Bruce Waltke, *Theological Word Book of the Old Testament* (Chicago, IL: Moody Publishers, 2003).

2. Richards, Larry, *Expository Dictionary of Bible Words* (Grand Rapids, MI: Zondervan, 1991).

Chapter 11
Manifesting God's Presence

1. *Vine's Expository Dictionary.*

TO CONTACT THE AUTHOR

IF YOU DO not know Jesus as your Lord and Savior, simply pray the following prayer in faith and Jesus will be your Lord!

> *Heavenly Father, I come to you in the name of Jesus. Your Word says, "Whosoever shall call on the name of the Lord shall be saved" and "If thou shalt confess with thy mouth the Lord Jesus, and shalt believe in thine heart that God hath raised him from the dead, thou shalt be saved" (Acts 2:21; Romans 10:9). You said salvation would be the result of Your Holy Spirit giving me new birth by coming to live in me (John 3:5–6, 14–16; Romans 8:9–11) and that if I would ask, You would fill me with Your Spirit and give me the ability to speak with other tongues (Luke 11:13; Acts 2:4).*

> *I take You at Your Word. I confess that Jesus is Lord. And I believe in my heart that You raised Him from the dead. Thank You for coming into my heart, for giving me Your Holy Spirit as You have promised, and for being Lord over my life.*

If you have just prayed this prayer, please let us know of your decision by contacting us at:

Faith Christian Center
3059 S. Cobb Drive
Smyrna, GA 30080
www.fccga.com